"*Summer of '94* is a fascinating exploration of found family and the importance of embracing what's important. With the fun thrills of scenery and the music scene of California in the '90s, this book is a fun adventure that will whisk you through its pages. Its compelling characters and complicated conundrums feel a lot like a drama from the era in which it is written, capturing all the best plot snapshots of a timeless '90s flick. You'll really enjoy this!"

—Hope Bolinger
Author of 20+ traditionally published stories such as
the Blaze trilogy and the Dear Hero duology

"Captivating and heartfelt, *Summer of '94* by C. Wolfe is a compelling coming-of-age story about a teenage girl raised by a single mother who longs to discover the truth about her father. Determined to fill the void in her life, Charlotte ventures into the glittering Hollywood rock scene—only to find far more than she bargained for. This beautifully written novel reminds us that what we think we want isn't always what we truly need. A highly enjoyable read and one I wholeheartedly recommend."

—Ane Mulligan
Award-winning author of the Georgia Magnolias series

"This is a page-turning story with characters that stay with you well after the end. Join Charlotte on her journey to California in her quest to find her real father, and hold on through her ups and downs amid the music scene of '90s Los Angeles, where 'dreaming was safe . . . reality was dangerous.' An exciting, compelling debut novel!"

—Peggy Wirgau
Award-winning author of *The Stars in April* and *To Outwit Them All*

A NOVEL

Summer of '94

A school paper turns into a search for the truth

C. Wolfe

Birmingham, Alabama

Summer of '94

Brookstone Publishing Group
An imprint of Iron Stream Media
100 Missionary Ridge
Birmingham, AL 35242
IronStreamMedia.com

Library of Congress Control Number: 2026902167

Cover design by www.BookCoverDesign.us

ISBN: 978-1-960814-24-1 (paperback)
ISBN: 978-1-960814-25-8 (eBook)

1 2 3 4 5—30 29 28 27 26

I want to thank my husband for listening to countless nights of me brainstorming. He encouraged me to get this book published. Also thanks to my mother and father for reading it, helping punch it up, and making this whole publishing process possible. Without them, this book may not have seen the light of day. Most important, I want to thank God for the creativity He's given me, for without Him there would be no book.

And lastly, my heartfelt thanks, dear readers, for making my thirteen-year-old self's dream a reality.

Chapter 1

Incomplete

A tear rolled down Charlotte's cheek as she sat next to the shallow creek. Her mind spun with endless thoughts of hopelessness. She had no idea what to do.

"Hiya, Lotty."

"Jason." Startled, she pressed a hand to her chest as her shaggy-haired best friend sat next to her in the soft grass.

His goofy grin creased his face as he nudged her with his shoulder. "I can never scare you. You looked like you were a million miles away." He noticed a wrinkled paper laying in her hands. "What's that?" He snatched the paper. "Is this our school paper from Ms. Talbot's class? She always does like to give out summer homework. What the heck are you doing with it? School's been out for like two weeks."

"I know. I haven't been able to finish it. Actually, I haven't been able to start it."

He snickered. "In all our seventeen years of living, you've never taken school so seriously before."

Her full lips pouted as her shoulders slouched.

"What's going on?"

"I feel like I've been totally sucker-punched in the gut." Her voice cracked.

"Because of our school paper?"

Charlotte read the typed prompt. " 'What do you want to be after you graduate?' I guess it's a simple question for some people but not for me. I feel so stupid." She wiped another tear, which escaped without her consent.

"Why do you feel stupid?"

She forced a laugh through watery eyes. "It's this dumb question. It's got me all confused."

"That's got you crying? This isn't like you."

"I don't know what I want to be when I grow up."

"That's okay. It's not that big a deal."

She faced him with crossed legs. "But it is to me. All my life there's been this *thing* inside me. Something I haven't been able to fully explain or even put into words. This thing, it's like a gaping hole in my chest, gnawing at me year after year, getting bigger and bigger. I don't think I can handle it anymore."

"I don't understand. This summer we should be coasting into our senior year. We've got one more year until freedom."

"That's what I dread."

"Why?"

Charlotte took a deep, shaky breath. "I've never known who my father is. You've known that."

"That's what this is about?"

She rolled her eyes. "You wouldn't understand."

"Sorry. I'm trying."

Charlotte chewed on a strand of her long brown hair while staring blindly at a croaking frog perched on a rock, jutting out of the rushing water.

"Charlotte, I promise I won't laugh."

"Did you do your paper?"

"Yeah. I finished it the weekend after school was out. I didn't want to even think about school or Ms. Talbot any more than I had to."

"And what do you want to be, Jason?"

His bright blue eyes lit up. "I want to work with computers. I programmed my own game last week, loosely inspired by *Wolfenstein* and *Doom*, which are revolutionary. The way *Doom* took pixelated 2-D objects and converted them into a 3-D space made me want to focus on shooters from the first-person perspective. These took me out of the arcade games like *Street Fighter* and *Mortal Kombat* and onto our computer at home. I find them fascinating and think they are going to be the future. My dad plays with Timothy and me sometimes. He still thinks it's a fad." A hint of annoyance came through in his voice.

"I don't have the luxury of playing with my dad. But I'm glad you know what you want to be when you grow up."

"It'll come eventually to you."

"Ugh, I'm not saying it very well." She turned Jason's wristwatch to check the time. "And I have that stupid women's potluck with Mom and Grandma here soon. I'm so not in the mood for it."

"Aren't Britney and the rest of her little clique going to be there too?"

She narrowed her hazel eyes at him.

"Sorry," he said, his mouth tightening. "They're so annoying."

Ever since they were kids, if Britney ever referred to him, which was rare, she'd call him *Jacey*. Both hated that nickname.

Throughout the years, Britney spread a few rumors about Jason, nothing too embarrassing, but the aftermath was always a nuisance. Every spring, they'd count down the days till summer, thankful that they ran in different circles.

"One reason I enjoy summer so much is not having to see Britney and them on a daily basis," Charlotte said as she scanned the words on the wrinkled paper for the millionth time.

Jason hesitated before asking. "Maybe you're thinking on this too hard? It's just a generic question."

"My mom is a real estate agent. Your dad is a copy editor for a company. Your mom works part time at the bank. My friends all seem so sure of themselves: Kim wants to be a ballet dancer with a ballet company because her mom was one. Olivia has already made demos and is fixing to move to Nashville to be a country singer like her uncle. You're going to be big and successful in computers because your dad showed you your first computer. He inspired you and pushed you to be the best. Me? I've got nothing. I don't know what I'm supposed to be."

"It's not a bad thing to not know yet."

"But I may never know. That's what I'm trying to say. I don't know who I am or where I come from. I'm nothing without knowing about my father's family." Tears trailed down her porcelain cheeks.

He frowned as he put a hand on her shoulder. "Is this what's been gnawing inside you? You don't know where you come from?"

She twirled a lock of her silky hair between her fingers. "I feel stuck. My mom refuses to tell me my father's name. In fact, she loses all control when I even bring him up."

"Wait. What?"

"Yeah. Growing up, I kept seeing all the other girls with their daddies, and I wondered, where's mine? Even my friends noticed. They'd ask about him. What does he do for a living? Where is he? Can I go visit him? Or if he's ever coming back. I didn't have answers for them. So, one day I asked my mom. I was about five or so. I riddled her with questions. But she'd never answer. She'd dismiss my questions or distract me by giving me a cookie or something.

"When I was at Olivia's seventh birthday party, her dad brought out the cake all lit up and sang a hilarious rendition of 'Happy Birthday.' He kissed her on top of her head and gave her the prettiest dress. Watching this, I felt a surge of jealousy and sadness. Later, when I got home and asked Mom the same curious questions about my own father, she outright yelled at me."

"What? Your mom never yells." Jason was shocked. "Remember that time when we got into heaps of trouble for swiping that pack of cigarettes and smoking them in your backyard? When she found us behind the bush, I thought for sure she'd lose it. Instead of yelling, she gave us that look. The kind of look that still turns my insides into quivering jelly. Sometimes, I wish she'd yell."

"No, you don't. It was awful. She blew up at me, telling me I didn't need a father and to stop asking. She said we'd done fine this far without one, and we'd be just fine going forward." Charlotte chewed on a nail. "I'd never seen her so upset. I felt bad for making her so angry, so I dropped the subject. I tried to believe what she said—that I'd be fine without my father."

"It's okay that you don't have a dad. Not everyone does."

"Well, I don't think it's okay. Neither does my grandma. I've never told you this. But do you remember my aunt Thelma's funeral?"

"Yeah, I do. She always smelled like moth balls."

"That's the one. We had people over for a reception."

"We played in the backyard, climbing the oak tree."

Her round face relaxed remembering how hard Jason tried to get a laugh from her that day. She wasn't too close to her great-aunt, so it wasn't difficult.

"After everyone had gone, my mom and grandma were cleaning up the kitchen from the reception. That's when I heard them arguing. They must have thought I was asleep. I crept up to my door and listened through the crack.

"I don't know what led to the fight, but my grandma said family is the most important thing. She even said a child needs a father figure in their life, and I had a right to know who my father was. It's important for growing up, she said. Even if he's dead, I had a right to know where I came from or I would never be whole."

"Does your grandma know your dad?"

"No. No one knows. I even asked my grandparents once. My mom hasn't told anyone. She disregarded everything my grandma said that night with a slew of words I had never heard her utter before. Grandma stormed out of the house." Charlotte blew out a puff of air. "I don't know what to think. A part of me accepts my life the way it is, but inside her words are itching and clawing at my insides. My grandma thinks there's something wrong with me."

"Well, she's wrong and shouldn't have said that. I think you're pretty special."

"Thanks."

They sat in silence as a gentle hush whispered through the dripping moss on the trees, and buzzing insects hovered over the water.

"What if she's right? What if I'm not whole until I find out who he is?" She took a deep, ragged breath. "What if my insides are twisting and clawing because I don't know where I come from or who I am." She groaned and brushed the tears from her eyes. "I don't know what to do, what to think, or what to feel."

"Well, then find out who your father is."

"What?"

"I can see this is something you feel is important. So find out who he is."

"Mom won't tell me."

"There are other ways. Find out on your own. I'll help you too. Look, you could write a fluff piece, generic on what you want to do with your life, and Ms. Talbot would give you an A as she usually does. Or you could find out who you really are."

A momma bird flew away from her nest as a slow smile appeared on Charlotte's face. A plan began to rise in her thoughts, hope surfacing for the first time in days. "You might be onto something. It's time to find out who I really am."

Chapter 2

Proven

Charlotte parked her bike near the red-bricked fountain. This decorative fountain drew tourists' attention as they drove through the storybook town. As if out of a canvas painting, she strolled down the paved walkway lined with historic lampposts and pink and white dogwood trees.

This park was a favorite of hers. She'd spent many occasions with her friends walking the trails and admiring the beauty. There were also many hideaways, which made great hangout spots far away from prying adult eyes.

Branching off to the right, she neared a shaded area with tables and chairs. The potluck group normally met in the city hall, but the air-conditioning had broken and couldn't be fixed in time for the luncheon. So they sweltered in the sticky heat, grateful for the gentle breeze offering some relief as they slowly sweat through their clothing.

"Welcome, ladies, to Oak Falls' Successful Ladies of Tomorrow luncheon where we believe in lifting one another up while preparing our next generation of young women to lead, to excel, and to represent Oak Falls well. Because you are here, our lovely daughters have the confidence to grow into the kind of young ladies who will succeed."

Charlotte rolled her eyes as Mrs. Aldridge welcomed everyone with their mouthful-of-a-club name. Taking a seat next to her mom, grandmother, and their friends, her mom squeezed her arm affectionately, a silent be good, and they listened to Mrs. Aldridge's introduction.

Charlotte exhaled quietly.

These luncheons were all the same: Sit still for an eternity and follow their social etiquette rules. Mrs. Aldridge droned on about the importance of everyone's place in the community and what this luncheon meant to every mother and daughter.

Her eyes drifted toward couples strolling together deeper into the park. How she envied them. They didn't have to sit through this nonsense. Mrs. Aldridge shifted into her talk about the future and who they were meant to become. It was intended to be inspiring. Charlotte felt nothing. How was she supposed to imagine her future when she didn't even understand her past?

They were given an icebreaker question to ask around the table. Once completed, the adults turned to gossiping about jobs, promotions, husbands, and whose baby was due next. It all blurred together and was painfully dull. Then came the inevitable questions tossed her way: How was school this year, Charlotte? Did you get good grades? Any thoughts on what you want to be when you grow up?

The last one always hit her in the pit of her stomach.

She wanted to talk about music. About the movie she'd seen four times already. But no one at her table wanted to hear about any of that. They wanted to discuss careers and the future.

"Lori." Her grandmother leaned over to Charlotte's mom, lowering her voice. "Why didn't you tell Charlotte to wear a dress?"

Lori adjusted the clip in her auburn hair. "Not now, Ma."

Sandwiched between them, Charlotte grimaced. "It's hard to ride my bike in a dress."

"Why didn't you come with your mother?" her grandmother asked.

"I had somewhere else to be beforehand."

A few people at the table cleared their throats, and the conversation ended right there. What Charlotte wanted to say was *not everyone can afford to be in a two-car family like you, Grandma*, but she swallowed it. That kind of honesty caused trouble.

A few tables over, she spied Britney and her friends, who giggled and squirmed in their seats. She made a mental note to steer clear of them today.

Making eye contact, she gave a tiny wave to her friend Olivia at the next table over. Great! Someone to talk to at this snore fest. Stifling a yawn, she repositioned her hands in her lap as Mrs. Aldridge took the microphone again.

Jason had told her to find her father. The thought lit a spark within her. She had a purpose now. A plan. Her stomach fluttered like it was filled with a swarm of butterflies. She couldn't wait to start.

Instead, she was here. Glancing at her mother's wristwatch, she counted the minutes until this speech ended and she could eat. Licking her lips, she eyed the tables filled with food just waiting to be eaten. Boy, Mrs. Aldridge loved to talk. Large dispensers of sweet tea glistened with sweat from the growing heat of the day. Even in the shade, her own shirt began to stick to her back. A tall glass of something iced and cold was calling her.

Finally, after another five minutes, everyone was encouraged to eat. Charlotte didn't waste a minute; alongside Olivia, she packed her plate with Southern delicacies and filled her cup to the brim. Guests naturally segregated by age and friend group. Her mom sought out Jason's mother while her grandmother settled in with the other silver-haired women.

"What have you been up to today?" Olivia asked in her slight Southern drawl as they slid into chairs at a table far from the adults.

"I hung out with Jason in Meadow Park. Now, I'm missing my afternoon shift at the video store for this."

Olivia rolled her eyes. "I know. As much as I love my momma, I hate these things."

"We see behind their ploy. Them trying to inspire us daughters to become successful women of tomorrow too. Well, this kind of inspiration ain't working." Charlotte giggled and scarfed down her boysenberry pie and its buttery, flaky crust. The sweet and tangy filling satisfied her taste buds. Boysenberry was her favorite. Yes, she ate her pie before her main course; that was the only way to do it.

"You and your pie." Olivia rolled her eyes with a smile. "There's other desserts you know."

"Pie is the best dessert there is, with chocolate chip muffins a close second."

While seated and eating, they gave warm greetings to a few women who walked past their table, engaged in conversation with the luncheon's guest speaker.

"If they want to inspire us, how about fixin' these events to make them more entertaining?" Olivia smirked. "I hate hearing about how important it is to be thinking long-term, networking, and laying the groundwork."

"Agreed."

"Stop having old Mrs. Freeman as the inspirational speaker. She's no more inspirational than a june bug dancing on a log."

"I second that. They could invite Johnny Depp or something."

"It has to be a woman."

"I wouldn't complain if they broke the rules."

"All I know is I'd be excited to come to one of these things if they had like Alyssa Milano or Winona Ryder or something."

"Totally," Charlotte affirmed through a mouth full of food. "Did you have a voice lesson today?"

"Uh-huh. Today Mr. Bowman had me sing an aria. I forget the name."

Charlotte gagged.

"One of these days, Charlotte, I'm going to get you to listen to opera."

"No way."

"It's actually quite beautiful. I learned a lot in my lesson."

"Never in a million years will you get me to change my mind. It's sooooo boring. But I'm sure you sounded great."

Olivia rolled her eyes and put the last forkful of potato salad in her mouth. The trash cans were situated near a cluster of trees, and they walked toward them with their plates when they heard muffled giggles and hushed whispers behind the trees.

Both girls paused.

". . . I can't believe she's even invited to these society luncheons."

Charlotte whispered as her plate hand hovered over the trash can. "Sounds like Britney."

Olivia nodded.

"It's supposed to be about successful women in the community, not sluts." The girls chuckled.

Charlotte and Olivia strained to catch who they were talking about.

". . . I'll tell you what. I heard my mom talking on the phone to Janice's mom that Mrs. Reynolds used to be some kind of slut or something."

Charlotte's eyes narrowed into slits and her mouth shrunk pencil thin. They were talking about her mom.

"Major slut."

"Why she showed her face in this small town knocked up, no husband, and broke is just plain ridiculous."

"My mom said Mrs. Reynold's parents were the only reason she hadn't been run out of the community."

"Maybe Charlotte's dad was a loser like her."

"Maybe he wanted nothing to do with them," one sneered.

"I wouldn't blame him. Charlotte's such a drag," Britney stated.

"I'd hate to be her."

"My mom pretends to be nice to Mrs. Reynolds, to be polite and all. But I've heard her call her a slew of words behind her back, and she called Charlotte a bastard."

"Truth hurts sometimes." Britney laughed.

Not being able to stomach another horrible word, Charlotte came out from hiding and stood before them, Olivia a few steps back.

All the girls hushed up and looked like kids caught peeking at their Christmas presents. After a few seconds, Britney squared up to

Charlotte. "What's your deal, Charlotte? Don't you have anywhere else to be?"

Charlotte stormed up to Britney and shoved the plate of leftovers into the mean girl's chest. Without breaking eye contact, she smeared it down Britney's brand-new designer dress, turning the pale green flowers into streaks of grease and uneaten potato salad.

Britney shrieked as her friends jumped back.

"I'll do worse if I ever hear you talking about my mother like that again." Charlotte spun around and stomped off.

Olivia scrambled after her. "That. Was. Awesome!"

Charlotte made a beeline for the drink dispenser, poured herself a glass, and downed it. Then another. Anything to keep herself from blowing her top.

"They said some awful things. I'm so sorry." Olivia placed a comforting hand on her friend's arm.

"Who said awful things?" Charlotte's grandmother came up beside them.

A few yards away, Britney emerged from behind the trees in tears, her friends hovering at her side. In a flash, her mom rushed up to her.

"Wonder what happened to Britney?" Lori asked while approaching, holding a lemonade.

"Never mind that, Lori," Grandma Reynolds said sharply. "Olivia, what did you mean by awful things?"

"Nothing, Grandma," Charlotte intervened, locking eyes with Britney across the lawn. She narrowed her gaze, daring her to speak. Britney wouldn't confess. She couldn't—not without outing her mother and her high society friends. It wouldn't be a good look.

Britney's mom followed her daughter's eyes and zeroed in on Charlotte. Straightening to her full height, the woman delivered a soul-sucking glare. On any other day, Charlotte would've shrunk to about two inches tall.

Usually, Dorothy Abernathy reminded her of Cruella de Vil from *101 Dalmatians*, fashionable and a terror to avoid. Not today. Her blood boiled too much to be intimidated.

Mrs. Abernathy marched up to Lori and jabbed a finger in her face. "Lori, in future, if you want to continue to be a part of these society luncheons and keep your standing in our community, learn to control your daughter."

Lori frowned. "What are you talking about? Charlotte? Did you make Britney cry?"

"Yes, I did," Charlotte stated with conviction.

Mrs. Abernathy turned up her nose. "My daughter deserves an apology. See that she gets it." With that, she stormed off, heading back to her daughter.

Whew. That wasn't as bad as Charlotte expected.

"What in the world is going on?" Lori demanded. "I can't believe you would behave like that."

Olivia took Lori's tone as her cue to leave.

"I hope you have a good explanation," her grandmother said, having forgotten all about her interrogation of what Olivia overheard.

Charlotte shrugged.

Lori put a hand on her hip and narrowed her eyes at her daughter.

Oh, no. The look.

"Well?"

"Mom, all I'll say is she deserved it, and I will not apologize."

"I think you will."

Charlotte crimped her lips and held her tongue.

"All we want is the truth," Grandma said.

Britney snatched her mom's BMW keys and took off. Curious and judgmental eyes from the ladies followed.

Straightening her back, Lori said from behind her big smile, "We'll talk about this later." Then she went to mingle and calm the tension.

Charlotte folded her arms over her chest.

"Charlotte," her grandmother gently asked, "what happened?"

"Britney's just psycho. Can we leave it at that?"

The drive home was quiet, too quiet.

Charlotte half expected her mom to say something or ask for an explanation. She didn't even look at her. Charlotte didn't know what was worse, getting scolded or the eerie silence. It wasn't until the front door closed that she got an earful.

"What got into you today, Charlotte?" Her mom dumped her purse and work binder on the table in their combined kitchen and dining room. "You are never one to initiate something like this, let alone toward someone as important in the community as Britney and her mother. I know they are not the most pleasant of people, but they have standing in our small town. Upsetting them can come back to bite us."

Grabbing a Coke from the fridge, Charlotte popped the tab. It fizzed and hissed. She gulped down a huge chug, and her eyes instantly watered. The carbonation burned her throat.

Lori crossed her arms. "Are you going to say anything?"

"I don't know what to say. Can we just get this over with, and you give me my punishment?"

"This isn't like you, Charlotte." She waited for her daughter to offer up something. "Well, if you want punishment, then here it is. You will go over to Britney's house and apologize to her for embarrassing her in front of half the town. You will also buy her a new dress from your video store paycheck."

"I can buy the dress, but I will not apologize."

"This isn't a negotiation."

"Mom, Britney and her friends are terrible and mean. They torture everyone in their path. Can you stop for one second and think about the idea that maybe what I did was in retaliation and not initiation?"

Lori braced her hands on the island. "Grandma said she overheard you and Olivia. That maybe Britney said something to you."

Charlotte ticked her finger on the top of the Coke can.

"Tell me what happened."

Charlotte couldn't. She couldn't do that to her mom. It would break her mom's heart if she knew what some of those women whispered about her. She stared at her Coke.

Lori leaned forward. "Charlotte, I cannot help you unless you talk to me."

Charlotte pursed her lips. "I don't want to talk about it right now."

"Okay, then when?"

"Mom, high school is hell with Britney in it. I do my best to stay away from her during the summer except for these luncheons you force me to."

"These luncheons are important for your future and mine. You know how hard I have to work to have a thriving practice. These women can make or break my business. I know Britney and her mother are snobs, believe me—I went to school with Mrs. Abernathy—but I cannot have you upsetting them."

Lori sighed as she poured herself a glass of wine and continued. "Look, Grandma seems to think that this is all Britney's fault. While I tend to agree with her, I still believe what you did was wrong." Taking a sip, she came around the island and held her daughter's arm. "I'll smooth things over with Mrs. Abernathy, but you will buy Britney a new dress."

"Okay."

"This better not happen again. Understood?"

Charlotte nodded.

Her mom kissed her cheek before taking her glass of wine to her bedroom.

Charlotte leaned on the countertop. What a relief. She didn't have to apologize. But what her mom had said struck a nerve.

Moving to the living room, she turned on the TV. Plopping onto the floor, she slid her legs beneath the coffee table's open lower shelf, the bottom edge brushing her shins. With her Coke can on the tabletop a few inches from her face, she snatched the clicker to switch the channel to MTV.

Nirvana's "Heart-Shaped Box" music video was playing. Charlotte stared mindlessly at Kurt Cobain playing his guitar in front of a red backdrop as she replayed her mother's words.

For years, her mom had used her career to brush aside her daughter's feelings. Work always hung in the balance. They had to do everything just right for the sake of her job, a job that pulled her mom further and further away.

They used to bake together. They'd talk about boys and movies and laugh over a buttery waffle or a chocolate chip muffin.

Everything was better with chocolate chips.

As time went by, those happy occasions were less frequent. Lately, they were nonexistent. Her mom always worked. Whenever they did talk, the conversation was about a sale or how to charm a new client in the community. Her mom's reputation was vital.

If her mom knew what those upstanding people thought of her, it'd break her heart.

Charlotte downed the remains of her carbonated liquid. To some extent, what people whispered about her mom was true. She was a single mom raising her kid in a community that found the subject less than favorable. But to go so far as to call her mom names and insult her character? Charlotte crushed the empty can in her grip.

Everyone at school seemed to have that traditional family dynamic. It was normal in this community. It was expected. Then came Charlotte and her mom—upsetting the status quo.

With each passing year, the longing for her unknown father became impossible to ignore. Overhearing Britney and her snobs intensified her inner doubts and made her gut twist and wrench. That persistent feeling of missing out on something forced her to wonder if she was somehow defective.

Charlotte got another Coke. It was that kind of day. Taking a large gulp, she stared hypnotically at Richie Sambora on top of a mountain in Bon Jovi's "Bed of Roses" music video. Her mind swirled and spiraled downward.

Bouncing her foot to the music, she brushed something on the bottom shelf of the coffee table. The family album. She hadn't looked through it in years. It'd be a welcome distraction.

Pulling it out and brushing the thin layer of dust off, she flipped through the first few pages. There were pictures of her as a baby with her grandpa and grandma. Many pages were of her and her mom.

There was a picture of her as a toddler being smothered in kisses by her mother. It was a good picture. Her mom's smile had warmth and beauty. With flowing, wispy hair and round brown eyes, her mom was a knockout. She was still pretty.

Charlotte flipped through a few more pictures, knowing she wouldn't see a single picture of her father. There was no trace or any mention of him. It was like he didn't even exist.

One picture caught her attention. She was about six or seven, having a picnic with her grandpa. Their outdoor adventures often included cloud watching, letting their imaginations run wild. She thought back to that particular day.

While lying on their backs, she had pointed to a cloud. "That one looks like a dragon's face. Oh! And that one is a turtle."

"I see a rabbit with a fluffy tail over there." Her grandpa gestured next to the turtle.

"That's not a rabbit."

"It isn't?"

"That's the turtle's robot friend."

Her grandpa laughed. "You have quite an imagination."

"Grandma says that too," little Charlotte said proudly, sipping juice.

"I bet you've imagined all sorts of things."

She bobbed her head.

"What if that cloud right there," he said pointing overhead, "was your father. What would he be doing?"

Charlotte studied the sky. "My father?"

"Yeah. Up there with the turtle and the dragon. What's he like?"

"Maybe he's an astronaut."

"That's good. He could be up there with the turtle and his robot friend. Have you ever thought anything else about him?"

"Like if he's a fireman or a policeman?"

"Sure. Or in any kind of way."

"Do you think he'll come back? Wouldn't it be great if he spent Christmas with us?"

"It sure would."

"I wish I could meet him. He'd tell me all sorts of bedtime stories and buy me lots of candy!"

Her grandpa put a hand over hers. "Stories about where we come from are a special thing. They help you understand yourself a little better."

She never forgot that.

Flipping through a few more pages, she stopped as a loose picture fell out. It was a Polaroid picture. The year 1974 was written on the back. Her mom would've been around seventeen—her own age.

Standing beside her mom was Aunt Becky. Aunt Becky wasn't really her aunt. She was her mom's childhood best friend. The two had grown up together in Oak Falls and were inseparable until Becky's dad landed a job clear across the country in California.

Charlotte's mom described it as awful, despite all the calls and letters. They were both so miserable that Becky's mom hosted them during the summers.

Those visits to California became a ritual. Charlotte's mom spent her summers there long after graduation until she got pregnant and stopped going.

They stayed in touch, but Aunt Becky's life was rooted in sunny California. Far from Oak Falls. Far away from messes like Britney Abernathy.

Charlotte studied the picture. Two radiant young girls, arms tossed around each other, smiling like they hadn't a problem in the world.

What could she say about her aunt? She was loud, fearless, and carefree. The kind of adult who tackled problems head-on. Whenever she breezed into town, life felt easier. Like problems could be handled instead of tiptoed around. And always handled with a laugh.

Her mom didn't know what to do about Britney except keep the peace. Grandma would only make things worse. But Aunt Becky always seemed to have answers.

Charlotte brushed the photograph with her fingertips. And right now, she needed one of those answers.

Chapter 3

The Search Begins

"Lotty, tell me it's true." Jason affectionately used the nickname he'd called her since they were kids and misspoke her name. It became a mishap that stuck ever since.

"What are you talking about?" While painting her toenails on her carpeted bedroom floor, she cradled a translucent phone between her shoulder and chin.

"You made Britney wear your food?"

Charlotte sighed. "Yeah, it's true."

Jason laughed hysterically over the phone.

"How did you hear about it?" Charlotte adjusted the phone against her neck.

"It's all over. A lot of our friends are on your side, by the way."

"I wish I didn't do it, but I'm also glad I did. She deserved it."

"What'd she do?"

Charlotte hesitated but then decided to give him a brief synopsis of the event.

He cussed through a clenched jaw. "Man, she got off lucky with just food on her dress. You could've given her a black eye. How dare she say those things about you and your mom."

"It's getting harder and harder to do nothing." The finishing stroke of dark burgundy nail polish glistened on her toenails. "The more people keep talking about my mom and me, the more I struggle with not knowing where I come from. I need to figure out who my dad is."

"What if your mom finds out what people are saying?"

She capped the bottle. "I don't want to upset her. I really don't. But I know she won't budge. The way I look at it is I can stay here in South Carolina, live my days working at Hollywood Video for the rest of my life, shelving VHS tapes of movies people want to watch—"

"With the gaping hole in your heart."

"Nicely put." Charlotte exhaled. "Or risk hurting my mom's feelings and finally figure out who I am and what I'm supposed to be." The stereo played "Heart-Shaped Box" in the background. "If she can't tell me who he is, then I'm going to have to find out on my own."

"And I'll do whatever I can to help."

"Thanks, Jase." She leaned against her bed. "Now, how would I go about finding out who my dad is?"

Jason chuckled. "You could start with your birth certificate."

"Birth certificate. Why didn't I think of that?"

"That's why I get paid the big bucks."

"How about I pay you in oatmeal cookies?"

"Deal. Do you know where it's at?"

"There's a few places it could be."

"I can't believe you're going to do this," Jason exclaimed.

"I know. This is exciting."

"Let me know if you need anything."

"I will."

After talking about the mundane events of the day a bit longer, Jason's mom reminded him of chores to be done. They hung up, and Charlotte stared at the collage of posters and article clippings, ranging from Johnny Depp to Bon Jovi, covering her walls. The first place she'd search was her mom's office. Everything important was in there.

Stepping carefully on her heels to avoid messing up her wet toenails, Charlotte skirted her clothes on the floor. Finding the house empty, she slipped into her mom's office. Filing cabinets lined one wall, and shelves of books filled another, with a large desk in the center.

Sitting in her mom's swivel chair, rocking from side to side, she scanned the visible contents. After finding nothing in the drawers, she tried the filing cabinet to her right. It was locked. Could her personal information be in there?

A search of the desk revealed a single key on a chain in the back of a narrow drawer. Placing it in the lock, she turned it.

Click. The cabinet drawer opened.

"Yes." She rifled through the neatly filed papers but no luck. It was information about her mother's business.

Brakes screeched in the driveway, causing Charlotte to jump like a kid with her hand in the cookie jar. Her mom was home. Slamming the cabinet shut, she threw the key into its original place and rushed out of the office before her mom came into the house.

She grabbed a can of Coke from the fridge as a pretense just as her mom entered the kitchen.

"Hey, Charlotte." Her mom set her purse on the dining table.

"Hey, Mom. How's it going?" Her heart thundered in her chest.

"Pretty good. Mr. and Mrs. Westbrook are finalizing their paperwork on their new house."

"You sold the Westbrooks the colonial cottage? Congratulations."

"Thank you." Lori did a little bow before pouring herself some water. "Six months of trying to find them the perfect place."

"Such picky people."

"They can't back out now. I guess they still could, but I won't let them." She chuckled.

"I'm sure they'll find something wrong with this one in time."

"People like them always do. But I know it's the right fit for them." Lori sipped her glass in triumph. "This calls for a celebration."

"Chocolate chip muffins?"

"You know me so well." Lori kissed her daughter on the head as she went to collect her purse.

"Coming up." The mixing bowl was located in the lower cabinet. "Hey, so I was looking through the photo album the other day. There's that picture of you and Aunt Becky in there."

Lori grinned from ear to ear. "I need to call her soon. It has been a while."

"When's the last time you two talked?" Charlotte continued her way around the kitchen grabbing baking supplies for the muffins.

"Oh, gosh. Must be a few months. We've both been so busy."

"You used to spend your summers in California with Aunt Becky, right?"

Lori nodded her head fondly. "Seems so long ago. We had lots of fun. Those were such good times."

"What'd you guys do?"

"Got into too much trouble." Lori chuckled. "The kind of trouble Grandma and Grandpa don't know and never need to know about." She zipped her lip.

"You? Getting into trouble? Doesn't seem like you." Charlotte grinned at her straitlaced mom, a twinkle in her eye. "I need details."

She cracked the eggs, added them to the sugar in the bowl, and whisked them together.

Lori sighed. "I would love to, but right now, all I want to do is slip into a bubble bath and let the last six months wash away." Squeezing her daughter's arm, she rounded the island and headed to the bathroom.

Charlotte paused mid-whisk. The conversation was just getting good. Surely her mom was going to help with the muffins or at least stay in the kitchen and talk like old times.

She should've known.

The bowl plopped on the counter with a clunk. Couldn't her mom spend twenty minutes with her and talk about anything and everything? The flour, other ingredients, then lastly the chocolate chips were added with frustration.

As she threw the muffin tin into the oven, her mind went back to her mom's office. There was a lockbox next to a printer. They hold important stuff. Maybe her answers were in there. She prayed they would be.

It wasn't even a shock at this point when her mom returned,

thanked her for the muffins, and took two into her bedroom for the evening to watch her programs, never once stopping to talk.

It was settled. After her mom went to sleep, she would sneak back into the office.

The lockbox waited.

She spent the rest of the evening in her room, pacing her floor, attempting to listen to music, and sitting on the edge of her bed, all the while glancing at the alarm clock on her nightstand. The red numbers ticked by. Midnight inched closer. Eyes glued on the clock, she drummed her fingers on her legs. Midnight struck. Springing from her bed with a thud, she grimaced, hoping her animated landing didn't wake up her mother.

She inched her doorknob to the right and poked her head into the dark hall. The house was quiet. No evidence of movement.

Her heart pounded.

Sticking a daring foot out into the hall, she froze. No reaction. She tiptoed down the hall, avoiding the squeaky spot on the floor, and was extra careful passing her mom's bedroom. Glancing over her shoulder to make sure the coast was clear, she slipped into the office.

A quiet sigh of relief.

The only source of light was the glow of the moonlight through the window. With hands stretched out, she cautiously went for the lockbox. It had a keypad—not a lock. This was a problem. Pursing her lips in thought, she then tried a few passcodes: birth dates and significant dates in her mom's life. None of them worked.

Easing into the swivel chair, she scanned all the contents on her mom's desk: a pencil holder, a desk lamp, a Rolodex, a miscellaneous holder, a neat stack of papers, and a letter opener.

Charlotte leaned forward.

The Rolodex.

An idea came into her mind.

She flipped through every single contact. In the middle of the thick stack was a blank card. Charlotte plucked it out and turned it over. On the back of the card were a few numbers.

Could this be it? Charlotte plugged in the numbers.

Click.

"All right," she said softly as she placed the passcode back into the Rolodex and opened the lockbox the rest of the way. Her hand hesitated before reaching inside. This was it. Either she'd find her birth certificate, with her father's name on it, or there'd be nothing. No answers.

She checked the door. Content with the silence, Charlotte hastily rifled through the stack of papers in the safe box. Her eyes still hadn't adjusted to the dark. With heightened exhilaration, she found her immunization and vaccination papers. Under a few more forms, she stopped at her birth certificate.

There it was. Hope stirred up within her.

She glanced at the name under the father's section. There was a name. With wide eyes, she read the words *Jesse Holt.*

His name had been easier to find than she'd hoped.

A creak interrupted her thoughts. Her mom's bedroom door opened.

Shoving everything back into the box, she shut the lid and crept to the office door to listen. Her mom shuffled into the bathroom and closed the door.

Charlotte snuck out and went into the kitchen for water, waiting by the faucet. The bathroom door opened, and her mom's footsteps faded down the hall. The door clicked shut.

She set the trembling glass down on the counter with an exhale. Hurrying back into her room, she cautiously lay down on her bed, avoiding the squeaky spring in her mattress. She stared at the ceiling.

Jesse Holt.

Her father's name. Finally.

It meant nothing to her. Not yet.

Chapter 4

Who Is Jesse Holt?

On Monday, Charlotte met up with Jason at his house to give him the scoop. They holed away in his messy bedroom, complete with Alice In Chains and Metallica posters haphazardly taped to the walls. The floor was his closet.

"Jesse Holt. Hmm. Doesn't ring a bell." Jason flicked back his hair from his eyes. "Hey, Mom," he called, and she came around the corner.

"What's up?" A perky woman in a T-shirt and jeans came to the threshold of his bedroom. Mrs. Hunter was polished, yet more than capable of going head-to-head with her two boys. She had even helped Charlotte out of a few tough scrapes while she was growing up.

When they were around nine, Jason dared her to climb the tree in their backyard. Charlotte accepted the dare and succeeded, but when climbing down, she fell—not too far but enough to scrape her elbow.

Mrs. Hunter didn't scold them. Instead, she bandaged Charlotte up and sent her on her way—but not before giving Charlotte a good dare she could use to get even with Jason. She was a pretty cool mom.

"Do you know of anyone named Jesse Holt?"

His mom scrunched her eyebrows together and stared into space before shaking her head. "It does sound vaguely familiar. But I can't put my finger on it. Why?"

"No reason. Just a name I heard. Thanks."

She disappeared somewhere in the house.

"Why did you do that?" Charlotte smacked his arm.

"If he had gone to school with them, she would've remembered."

"She's gonna say something to my mom."

"I doubt it. A potential old classmate is useless information. If I said he might be your father, she'd spread that to all her friends in no time."

Charlotte wasn't super convinced but had to trust Jason's knowledge of his mom.

He brushed his hair back again in thought, then scrambled out of his room to grab the phone book. Plopping onto the floor, he brushed aside a pile of jeans and flipped to the *H*'s. He scrolled down with his finger to find a *Holt, Jesse*. "There's only one in the area."

"It can't be this simple."

"Maybe it is." Jason shrugged and retrieved the cordless phone from their kitchen.

Charlotte's finger hovered over the buttons. With a little help from Jason pushing her finger on the first number, she finished dialing.

A feminine voice spoke on the other end. Charlotte cleared her throat. "Hello, I was looking for a *Jesse Holt*. Would he be home?"

They listened as the voice explained *she* was in fact Jesse Holt. Thanking her for her time, Charlotte hung up. "Not that easy."

"Okay. Next stop is the library."

Pedaling on her bike and Jason riding his skateboard, they made their way to the local library. They arrived in no time, secured their rides, and went inside, smiling at the polite greeting they received from the librarian. Gathering several stacks of phone books from the librarian, they made their way to one of the tables.

"Hey, Charlotte." A friend of theirs from school approached.

"Hi, Mindy."

"That was so awesome what you did to Britney."

She grimaced. "Thanks."

"I'd never have had the guts to stand up to her like that," Mindy said, then went on her way.

Charlotte sunk into her chair and buried her face in her arms.

"I'm going to need to lay low for a good long while. I don't need any more attention. It'll just turn up the heat on Britney and force her to retaliate."

"Serves her right," he muttered.

"I'm on thin ice with my mom about the subject. I'm totally lucky she's going to smooth things over. I just had to fork over seventy bucks cash this morning to replace that dress."

"Who spends seventy bucks on a dress?"

"I know, right? That's like sixteen hours of work at the video store wasted." Charlotte blew the hair out of her face. "This situation just can't turn into anything major."

"It'll all work out," Jason said as he arranged the phone books on the table.

Charlotte scooted close to him, close enough that their shoulders touched.

He flipped through the pages.

"What are we doing exactly?" she asked.

"I figured we'd start with these phone books. The library has many for local and the neighboring states."

"Right. This way we look in the white pages to see if there are anymore *Jesse Holt*s outside of Oak Falls."

Both pouted at the daunting stacks.

"The library also keeps local and out-of-state directories for businesses and residents. If your mom knew a *Jesse Holt*, he's got to be in one of these. We just got to make the connection."

For several minutes, they scanned rows of names.

"Look." Jason pointed. "There's three *Jesse Holt*s in North Carolina." He cleared his throat as she leaned in to look at his column.

"Great." Charlotte grabbed a pencil and notepad from her handbag. "Write their phone numbers and addresses down. We'll start a list of candidates." Another few minutes went by as she flipped through an out-of-state phone book. "Here's several in Georgia," she said.

"How many are there?"

She slouched. "Quite a few."

"Just keep collecting their information for now."

"This is going to be an expensive phone bill." She shook her head at the growing list.

"Is your plan to call them up and ask if they're your dad?"

"Well, yeah."

"He may not even know you exist."

"Oh, yeah. Hadn't thought of that. What do you reckon I do?"

Jason leaned back in the chair and shook his mane. He stared up at the high windows pouring in morning light. "Okay. This is what we'll do. We'll narrow the list down. Their age, job, if they're married. If the timeline doesn't fit your birthday, we'll rule them out. Lastly, we'll look for a connection. Your mom had to know this guy."

She nudged him. "You're smart."

They spent the rest of the morning at the library combing through the out-of-state phone books and business directories, jotting down every *Jesse Holt* they could find.

Glancing at the large clock hanging over the front desk, Charlotte yawned. "I have to grab some lunch before my afternoon shift. I guess those VHS tapes won't shelve themselves."

"I'll keep working on this and talk to you later with any updates."

"You're the best, Jase." She tousled his shaggy hair.

All afternoon at Hollywood Video, her mind spun with possibilities from their investigation. She wished the stack of tapes were the phone books so she could actually help Jason.

With arms full, she wove through the narrow aisles, the air thick with stale popcorn and plastic sleeves. She slid *Tombstone* into an empty spot on the shelf, trying not to knock over its neighbor.

Sometimes this job was such a bore, but the monotony was broken up whenever a customer wandered past or stopped to ask a question. The money was good, covering summer expenses she wouldn't have been able to afford otherwise.

With the last VHS tape in her arms, she tucked *Sister Act* into a vacant space and headed back toward the front counter.

"Charlotte." Her name barked across the store cut through her thoughts. "You put *Tombstone* in the romantic comedy section." The manager stomped down the aisle, waving the VHS tape in his hand as he placed it in its proper home.

"Sorry," she muttered.

"And *Sister Act* is not a horror. Get your head out of the clouds."

Charlotte walked the aisles again, checking for misplaced tapes. But honestly, she didn't care.

Butterflies fluttered wildly in her stomach. Were any of the *Jesse Holts* on their list her father? Finding him took up all of her mental capacity. There was no room left in her brain to care whether *Sister Act* belonged on a specific shelf.

The hands on the clock ticked by.

Too slow.

She hoped Jason found something. A few friends rented videos and, of course, congratulated her for her actions at the women's luncheon. It was only a matter of time before Britney exacted her revenge.

Charlotte put away the last of the returns when the doorbell jingled. Her face brightened as Jason walked in, cradling his skateboard under his arm.

"Jase, what are you doing here? Why am I asking that? Who cares? Did you find anything out?"

"Hold your horses. I may have something." His eyes danced.

"Don't be cruel." She shoved him.

"Okay, I do have news."

"Good news? Bad news? Oh, gosh. I can't handle this. Don't tell me yet. Hold on. Let me clock out." Charlotte wrote her time on the timecard. Not waiting to hear a goodbye from her boss, she grabbed Jason's hand, and they raced out of the store.

Walking her bike beside Jason, they took the route toward their homes. "You have news. Fingers crossed, it's good. Oh, please let it be good."

"Several of the Holts from North Carolina and a few in Georgia are all crossed off our list."

Charlotte blinked a few times. "Really? Huh. How do you figure?"

"Well, I called them. Some were women, and the others had never been to Oak Falls in their lives."

"How many long-distance calls did you make? That's expensive."

"Nah, it wasn't much."

"Jase." She whacked his arm. "Tell me how much it was, and I'll repay you."

"Don't worry about it." He playfully tugged at her hair.

Charlotte knew she wouldn't win by protesting. Visions of baking him several batches of oatmeal cookies ran through her head. She walked her bike a few more steps before continuing, "Okay, so where does that leave us?"

Jason stopped walking. "You're not going to believe this. But one of the librarians found two highly possible *Jesse Holt* contenders. One's in entertainment. I call him Mr. Entertainment. The other's in health care. Mr. Tennessee."

"Really? Wow."

"She brought over two folders with clippings about them in each folder. News articles. Interviews. Bios. Then she said she found microfilm on both and led me to a projector. I spent all afternoon scrolling through old articles. I asked her for any and all films she had on the both of them. I think she got sick of me after a while."

"I love those things," Charlotte interjected. The microfilm readers were like a slide-show projector. They had a rotating handle that would flip to the new slide of a newspaper or article being researched or read. She liked to spin the handle.

They turned left onto Elmer Road, a suburban street lined with quaint houses and ancient trees.

"Who do you want to hear about first?"

"Start with Tennessee."

"Well, Tennessee is a health care executive in Nashville. He's made the headlines several times for his high-profile lifestyle. From the few tidbits I could find, he dated Miss South Carolina many years ago. There was even a picture of her and him standing by the Oak Falls welcome sign."

"No way."

"And he still looks pretty good for his age."

"Maybe he charmed my mom after ending it with Miss South Carolina. Gross." She wriggled her shoulders.

"Only thing is he is about fifty-four or so. Born in 1940."

"Would have been almost forty when he had me. My mom was twenty. Major age gap. But I guess it's not out of the realm of possibilities."

"Like you said. Gross."

"Totally. I just don't see it. They don't run in the same circles. And I don't remember her ever saying she went to Nashville."

Jason flicked his hair. His blue eyes sparkled. "Which brings us to Mr. Entertainment."

"Tell me about him."

"You're not gonna believe this."

"Tell me. Tell me. Tell me."

"He's a musician."

"A musician? Cute, I guess."

"Charlotte, I'm not gonna lie, he seems like a good candidate."

Charlotte stopped in her tracks. "Really?"

"He's about thirty-nine or so, born late June 1955, and has been in some rock band since the '70s and '80s."

"He would've been pretty young."

"Around twenty-two. Not impossible. Better than the twenty-year age gap of Tennessee."

"True."

"I saw several pictures of him from the newspaper articles, and I reckon you kind of look like him. You could pass as his daughter, I guess. You both have one dimple on the right side of your face. Same big smile. Big teeth," he teased.

She crinkled her nose and jabbed his side with her finger.

"And you want to know the connection?"

"More than anything."

"He's from California. Didn't you tell me your mom spent her summers as a teen in California?"

Charlotte's round hazel eyes widened. "Oh, my gosh. She did. Many summers."

"Maybe your mom was a fan of the band, and they dated or something."

"Oh, this is so good and weird."

"So weird."

"But good."

They came to a stop sign at a rural intersection. Here they parted ways. "Hey, meet me at the library tomorrow afternoon. We can do some more digging into California."

"All right. Hey, Jason. Thanks for all of this." She gave his arm an affectionate squeeze.

Jason cleared his throat, then shook his shaggy locks. "Don't—don't uh, worry about it." Jumping onto his skateboard, she marveled at his skill as he pushed himself to an impressive speed down the road.

Charlotte squished into her purple pillow and stared at the popcorn ceiling. A musician. It wasn't a terrible idea. To be honest, though, this particular occupation never crossed her mind as a possibility.

What kind of musician?

Did he play in his little band with his buddies in clubs around the city?

Charlotte pursed her lips. It wasn't ideal, but she had to admit, this musician was way more plausible than Tennessee. Her mom spent a significant amount of time on the West Coast. Could their paths have crossed? Did he see her in the crowd, and was it love at first sight?

The more she dwelled on this musician, the more questions she had.

Who was Jesse Holt?

She had to know everything and anything about him, and tomorrow she would get these answers.

Chapter 5

Here We Go

The next morning, Charlotte rode her bike to the town's record shop. If this musician was anything, maybe his band's records made it into the Vinyl Vault. It was a long shot, but she couldn't just sit at home waiting until she had to meet Jason.

Her first step in her own investigation was Jesse Holt's music. Bouncing into the store, she said passing hellos to some of her school friends who were purchasing the latest music.

She started toward the rows of records, then stopped. In all her excitement, she had forgotten to ask Jason the name of Jesse's band.

An employee clicked a mouse, eyes glued to the screen.

"Excuse me, do you have any CDs of a musician named Jesse Holt?"

"Jesse Holt?" He leaned on the counter.

"He was in some rock 'n' roll band based in California."

He grew a huge smile, guided her to the rock section, and presented a large album. "Let me introduce you to the best summer of your life."

Caravan.

Why did that sound familiar?

All the members on the cover were in various poses. It dripped with '70s vibes. Several sported long hair, and some wore fringed leather jackets or vests. One member wore a beaded tribal necklace with wolf teeth, and another displayed their T-shirt with the band's name across his chest.

"They have a total of eleven albums, seventeen hit singles in the Top 40 charts, and several greatest-hits albums. Several reached gold and platinum, and some even double platinum."

Charlotte couldn't peel her eyes away from the record cover. They were way more famous than her mental image of a side-hobby, garage-band group of guys trying to make it. These guys were legit rock stars. Their name did sound familiar. Had she heard some of their songs before? Most important, which one was Jesse Holt?

"They are a hard rock, funk rock band with an edgy sound and great lyrics. Throw in some blues and metal, and you have Caravan. Danny's got wicked vocals, and Jesse has amazing guitar licks." He pointed to the guitarist, and Charlotte's eyes lingered on him.

Wearing the tribal necklace over his vest, he was undeniably handsome. His youthful face and piercing brown eyes made him the type of man a lot of girls would go crazy for back in the day. If her mom was any type of normal teen girl, she would have found him attractive.

"Are you a new fan?"

"Yes, I'm needing new music."

"Oh, cool. Then I might suggest checking out their other albums." He handed her four vinyl records as she continued to stare at the man who might be her father. "I don't seem to have all their records, but I know I have a few of their CDs."

"I'll take all you got." She tucked her prized possessions under her arm.

"Nice." All the way to the CD section, he talked more about the history of the band and their established sound. "They were all young guys: eighteen, twenty. Starting out playing dives and nightclubs all up and down the West Coast. They knew their sound and put their stamp in the music industry. Their earlier stuff has a flare of psychedelic rock, and you can hear their transition into the '80s. They tested the waters with pop, but it doesn't take away from their quality. Danny, he's got some vocals that'll blow your mind. Jesse's guitar and Danny's voice could line up just right and give you goosebumps," he stated. "I went to one of their concerts when I was a kid. Whoa man. It was epic. One of the best shows I've ever seen." Placing the last CD in her arms, he said, "There you go."

"Great, thanks."

"I'll get you right over here." He went behind the counter and started scanning the music.

"You said you went to one of their concerts. Do you know if they still play together?"

"Um, I think they're finishing up a tour. Though I don't know anything further than that."

Twenty years and still together. Impressive.

"Thank you." Charlotte took her bagged music and left the shop. Pedaling fast, she couldn't wait to hole away in her bedroom and listen to the music. This was an important moment, and she wanted to experience it alone before sharing it with Jason.

The summer heat caused perspiration to trickle down her back. The cool breeze was her only relief, and there was barely any. Even though she was sweltering, an ear-to-ear grin creased her face.

Biking down a long stretch of picturesque colonial homes, she stuck her feet out straight and outright laughed. Every limb tingled with excitement. Some familiar faces from school came riding their bikes in the opposite direction. They exchanged waves and shouted hellos before continuing their separate ways.

Turning down her street, she instinctively stood as she pedaled to avoid every bump from the brick road against her tires. She came to a stop in front of her historic fairy-tale home. That's how she always thought of it, a fairy tale. It looked like a dream with creamy white siding and forest-green decorative shutters by every window. A large oak tree in the front lawn shaded the house, and pink and purple flowers and shrubs nestled in front of their large, cozy porch.

Charlotte tossed her bike on the front lawn and raced inside. Slamming the door shut, she flopped onto the floor, pulled out the collection of music from the bag, and picked up the vinyl on top.

The cover read *Here We Go*, and the album was released in 1980. The employee said it was one of their most popular albums, reaching number two on the music charts. Impressive. Number two on the music charts was hard to achieve. She secured her door and hooked up her headphones before placing the needle on the grooves.

A few seconds of crackling white noise filtered through her headphones. Then the music began. A heavy guitar intro played as she stared at Jesse Holt on the cover. He was dressed in faded jeans, white sneakers, and a fitted shirt.

Her foot bounced to the drum beat as the bass vibrated her insides. Then the singer started. He was good. Amazing even. But the guitar's syncopated melodic tones were leagues above anything else. The harmonized chorus came in, and when the singer's voice trailed off, the guitar solo began.

He shredded an edgy guitar solo.

Fast.

Intricate.

Wild.

The singer came back in and harmonized with the guitar in a vocal and instrumental duet.

She checked the song list, and this was the title track, "Here We Go." While listening to the entire record, she gasped at recognizing one or two of the songs. They had played on the radio. On another album, she recalled two songs, "Lover in Sunlight" and "Dazed." It was funny how she never knew the band's name.

Rifling through the other records and CDs, she paid attention to the pictures and followed along with the lyrics on the sleeve. Every line from the CD booklets was read.

Within the pages was a candid picture of them all laughing. She smiled. Jesse's sunshine smile was infectious. Turning toward her floor-length mirror, she attempted a smile to see if there was any resemblance. Jason was right. They both had big mouths with long teeth, and when they smiled, both their noses wrinkled. Even the dimple was the same.

The rest of the morning was spent listening to their music until she happened to glance at the time, twelve thirty.

"Oh, my gosh!" She had to meet Jason at the library soon.

All the albums and CDs were shoved under her bed. She made sure there was no visible trace of their music. About to leave the room, she stopped. Removing the record from the turntable, she returned it to its sleeve and pushed it under the bed to join the rest.

So close. It would've been game over if her mom found their music in her possession.

Slapping together a PB&J sandwich and stuffing it into her mouth, she grabbed a Coke from the fridge, then raced outside. It was hotter than blue blazes as she snatched up her bike and put the can in her basket.

Once there, she flew off her bike and entered the library to find Jason already at the computer.

"Hiya, Lotty." His face brightened as she neared.

"I went to a record shop this morning and bought everything I could find of their music. They are a legit rock 'n' roll band, like extremely popular. We've even heard a few of their songs on the radio. I never put two and two together. I mean, I wasn't too keen at first about being a musician's"—she glanced around before saying the last word—"daughter. But I'm totally warming up to the idea."

"Whoa. Slow down. Say that again? You did what?"

"Jesse Holt is a massive rock star. Several of his band's albums are in the Vinyl Vault, and I bought and listened to them."

"That's awesome. Are they any good?" he teased.

"So good. Remember that time when we drove to Kim's house to pick her up for that dance recital she had?"

"And I had to swerve to avoid that jerk of a driver who cut us off and slammed on his brakes. Oh, yeah, I remember."

"You did a great job of saving your mom's car. Anyway, their song 'Dazed' was playing on the radio when we pulled into Kim's driveway."

He pursed his lips and shook his head. "I don't remember."

"Yeah, probably not. You were still cussing that driver out all the way to the dance recital."

They spent the rest of the afternoon huddled in front of the microfilm reader, scrolling through old reviews. Some were favorable and others not so much, but that was typical for critics, they thought. The same librarian who'd helped Jason the previous day suggested the entertainment magazines, informing them there were magazines dating back almost thirty years.

Thanking her, they went to the section. Rows and rows of magazines, every category neatly labeled. They zeroed in on music.

Charlotte couldn't believe it. Their own library had old rock magazines on Caravan—*CIRCUS*, *CREEM*, and *Rolling Stone* issues that had been forgotten for years. Caravan's name was plastered on some of the covers. Headlines. Photos. Full spreads.

Sprawled out on a faded red couch against the brick wall, they poured through issue after issue. Several articles centered on their front man, Danny Racer. It was hard to admit, but he was even better looking than Johnny Depp.

Then she saw Jesse Holt.

She turned the pages slowly, studying his face. He was tied with the singer in the looks department, a stronger profile with slightly harsher features. But the idea of lumping her supposed father into the heartthrob category made her insides lurch upward. It was all just so weird.

Did he know she existed?

From his end of the couch, Jason glanced up from a *Teen Beat* issue on Jesse Holt. "There's some wild stories in here. It's got to be all made up."

"You're no fun." She leaned across the couch for him to see her column. "Look, it says here Jesse Holt is a tough guy and protects his friends almost to a fault. He once beat a bully up at school, sticking up for the bullied kid."

"Probably fake to give him a tough-guy image." Jason laughed and stood, replacing his magazine.

Scrunching her nose at his lack of imagination, she read a "Jesse Holt—On the Spot" page. "This one says he likes to ride his motorcycle when he's not performing, plays at nightclubs any chance he can get, and likes cheeseburgers and chocolate shakes. He has a temper but also has a tender side."

Jason made exaggerated gagging noises as he sank on the green carpet.

Charlotte barely heard him. If this man was her dad, why had he left?

"'Caravan plays to a sold-out arena tour as their fifth album, *Here We Go*, soars to number two on the charts in the United States. The only question now is not *if* but *when* they reach number one.'"

Joining him on the floor, she leaned against the bookshelf. "That's their *Here We Go* album. Just listened to it. It's so good."

He scanned farther. "'Caravan defies the mainstream by writing music which isn't widely commercially accepted.' Whoa, the critics are attacking them mercilessly: 'lack of originality, aggressive, and failure to understand what music is.' Yeesh. Brutal."

She scoffed. "All lies. I've heard their music. Those critics need their hearing checked. Wouldn't it be cool if they are still touring?"

Jason snapped his fingers and headed for the periodicals near the front desk.

"What are you thinking?" she asked while following.

"If they're touring, it'll be in here." Picking up the latest issue of *SPIN*, he turned toward the back pages. "Look! Here they are. Caravan. They're touring. It says, 'The band kicks off its summer leg with a brief Santa Monica Pier set in June before settling into a run of California dates later this summer.'"

Charlotte read it once. Then again. California. June. Her pulse quickened. He wasn't just a photograph or a name on a birth certificate. He was out there. What would happen if she met him? Would he accept her? Or worse, reject her?

"He's our strongest connection. I've got to know if it's him. I've got to meet him."

"I don't know how you can do that. It's not like you can just fly out there to California."

Closing the magazine, Charlotte's eyes widened with a growing smile. "I might have an idea. I'm gonna call Aunt Becky."

That evening, her mom came home with a surprise pizza and a movie. Charlotte was shocked but didn't complain. Any chance for time with her mom was relished. Her mom wanted to spend time with her, and she was on cloud nine.

The beginning of *The Princess Bride* started. They were together in front of the television. Total bliss. Charlotte didn't even mind hearing about her mom's day. She wanted to grill her mother about her father, but knowing she'd only get frosty friction, she stuffed her face with pizza instead.

Unfortunately, this dream night didn't last long. During Princess Buttercup's capture, her mom dropped some new information. "So I have some kind of bad news. My schedule has been filling up. I'm real sorry, but I'm going to be extremely busy during the summer. I know we talked earlier this year about going to Disney World, but honey, I don't see it happening now. I'm sorry."

She should've known. This was pity pizza.

Charlotte offered a weak, appeasing smile. "That's all right. You're doing what you have to do." Besides, she hadn't had high hopes for their Disney trip anyway.

"Do you have any big summer plans? Hanging out with Jason or Olivia or Kim?"

"Funny you should ask." And as if it couldn't have been timed any better, the phone rang.

Lori sprung up from the couch to answer the phone. "Hello, Lori speaking." Her face lit up, "Becky!? How the heck are you? This is a surprise."

Opportunity was on the phone. Her plan was coming to fruition, and all that stood in her way was her mom's approval.

"It has been too long, hasn't it? Oh, it's so good to hear your voice.

What have you been up to lately? Any exciting summer photo shoots?" Lori listened.

Charlotte chewed on a strand of hair, legs bouncing.

Her mom's face slowly dropped into a furrow.

"You want Charlotte out with you for the summer? I know. It's been a while since the two of you hung out. . . . It would be fun, but this comes as quite a shock. . . . Yeah, I guess living on a whim was always your style." Lori locked eyes with her daughter. "Charlotte, do you want to go to California?"

Charlotte nodded emphatically.

Lori's brow was still in the frown position. "How long do you want to have her? Six weeks? That's a long time. . . . You sure it's not an imposition?"

Her mom hadn't said no yet.

A good sign.

"Well," Lori said as she threw her hand up, "I guess if it's not too much trouble, Charlotte is more than welcome to stay with you for the summer."

Charlotte's stomach did inward somersaults and handsprings.

"Yes, you and I need to have a reunion sometime. . . . Charlotte and I will work out the plane tickets. Okay."

What just happened? Her mom agreed. A flurry of emotions threatened to escape. Bursting onto the front porch, her body shook with uncontrolled fits and giggles.

"This is happening," she whispered. She was going to find her father. It was truly happening.

For the first time in her life, that hole inside her didn't ache so much. She had a chance to get answers, and nothing could stop her now.

Saying her goodbyes, her mom hung up the phone. The screen door screeched as Lori came onto the porch. "I guess you're going to California."

Charlotte barreled into her. "Thanks, Mom."

"What made you call Aunt Becky?"

"I don't know. I saw that picture in the photo album. I hadn't seen her in a while, and what better place to spend my summer vacation than California. I love Aunt Becky."

"I love her too. I hope you two have fun, but not too much fun." Lori held up a warning finger.

"I promise." Charlotte crossed her heart.

"Aunt Becky—she's a good woman, but she can still party like it's the '70s. You might have to keep her in check."

Charlotte was bursting at the seams. "I'll do my best."

"You're going to have so much fun. I'm a bit jealous," she teased.

"I'll take lots of pictures and send postcards and stuff."

"You better." Lori hugged her. "I'm going to miss you."

"I'll miss you too."

That evening her mom helped her make an airline reservation over the phone. The earliest flight was for Friday morning, giving her a few days to pack and say goodbye to her friends.

Sleep didn't happen at all that night. It was spent packing and repacking. With her empty suitcase next to her on the floor, piles of clothes strewn about, she held one of Caravan's albums in her hands. While her mom handled summer obligations, Charlotte was determined to get answers.

The day before her flight, Charlotte told Jason to meet her at their spot along the hiking trail at Meadow Park. Arriving early, she sketched in her notebook to keep her mind from spinning, and of course, drew one of Caravan's album covers.

The chirping birds and humming insects helped calm her excitement. With every stroke, she worked to get each detail correct. The frogs croaked to her left, followed by a few splashes from the creek. The trees reminded her to be still with their whispered *shhhhhh* when the wind gently rustled their leaves.

By the time Jason arrived, she had completed the detailing on Jesse Holt and Danny Racer.

"Wow, that's really good." Jason took up a seat and shook back his hair. "Okay, fill me in. What time do you leave tomorrow?"

"I need to be at the airport at eight thirty in the morning. I can't believe I'm spending the summer with Aunt Becky. I also can't believe I spent half my life savings. But I don't care. It's all worth it."

"How did you break the news to Gerry?"

"He wasn't too happy I quit—and without a longer notice. Don't think he'll take me back when senior year starts."

"Eh, you'll find another job."

"I'm not worried. My mind is now trying to figure out how to get in touch with the band." She slumped.

Jason's silly grin spread across his face.

Charlotte straightened. "What? What did you do, Jase? You're grinning like a Cheshire cat."

"You're going to owe me so big."

"What?! Tell me. Tell me."

"What if I told you I got ahold of their manager's number."

"You did what?!" She shoved him. "How on earth did you do that?"

"Long story short, I have a connection out there and, with some arm twisting, I got the band manager's number."

"Jason Hunter, you are full of surprises."

"And I've already talked with the manager. I told him I was with Harrison High, some school I looked up out there. I said Charlotte Reynolds is an aspiring journalist wanting to cover the band for the summer as a way to defend musical arts staying in our school system."

Charlotte frowned. "The manager won't buy that."

"He did."

Her mouth gaped open like a fish. "What?!"

"They eat stuff like this up. Whenever bands like them are on MTV, they are always fighting for music to stay in school. Their manager said they've done stuff like this before and would be happy to have you interview the band at the Pier shows for your article."

"Jason, I don't know how to write a serious article."

"You're not really going to."

"Oh, right."

"This gives you the opportunity to hang out with the band, ask them questions, get backstage passes, and see if Jesse Holt is your dad."

Her stomach fluttered. "This is so crazy. It just might work. You've thought of everything."

"I know how important this is to you."

Charlotte squealed and hugged him tight. "I'm going to California! The only thing I'm sad about is ditching you for the summer."

"It'll be boring around here without you, that's for sure. But I'll be all right. I hear Hollywood Video is hiring," he teased. "How hard is it to put a VHS tape on a shelf? Then I'll skateboard with Tanner and Clint. I'll have plenty to keep me busy."

At seven thirty in the morning, Jason pulled up in Charlotte's driveway, then drove her to the airport. They blasted Caravan in the car, windows down and heads bobbing.

Between songs, Charlotte reasoned, "You know, this is probably a good thing. Maybe being gone will take the heat off me and the whole Britney thing."

"From what I heard, she's still fuming. Even after getting a new dress."

"My mom did some sweet talking with Mrs. Abernathy, but Britney isn't one to easily forget."

"Now she can't do anything with you not here. I bet she'll enjoy hearing you're spending your time in sunny California." Jason laughed as he pulled into a parking spot. He carried Charlotte's luggage into the airport and waited with her as she confirmed her tickets and checked her bags.

As they walked to boarding, he said, "Okay, you remember my cousin, Matt?"

"Of course, I remember Matt. It's impossible to forget someone who never seemed to like me. He was always so serious."

"He doesn't like anybody. That's just his way."

"It probably didn't help that I tried way too hard to get him to break."

Growing up, Charlotte had made it her mission to get Jason's cousin to crack a smile. She tried jokes at potlucks or over-the-top greetings at the grocery store—anything to break that stony frown. All she received was a cold shoulder. She never understood it, especially because his mom was so bright and warm, and his younger brother was always laughing.

"I told Aunt Heather you were headed out there and that Matt better be nice. She already called him and 'softened him up.' "

"Glad I'll have one familiar face out there besides Aunt Becky. Doesn't he do something with bands?"

"He's a local roadie."

"That's right."

"And he'll meet you at the side of the stage at the Santa Monica Pier show tomorrow. He'll let you backstage and introduce you to the manager."

"Perfect."

"Between his mom and me, we made him promise to keep a lookout for you so you shouldn't have any problems."

"This still feels like a dream. I keep pinching myself."

"Oh, and this is for you." Jason handed her a medium-sized notebook. "For you when you interview the band. Inside I wrote down questions to ask them, ones I've heard on MTV or read in articles and such."

"This is incredible. Thank you so much." She gratefully brushed her fingertips over the sleek notebook, then clutched it protectively. "Jason, you've done so much for me. How can I repay you?"

"Get me a signed T-shirt or CD or something."

"You got it."

"Send me postcards updating me about everything, and let's call once a week. But you better call me after you meet him."

"You'll be the first to know." Giving him one last hug and saying goodbye, she boarded the plane. This was happening. She was flying across the country to find her father.

Chapter 6

First Encounter

Charlotte stepped onto California soil at LAX and paused amid the sea of people. Unsure where to go, she barely avoided a man racing to his destination.

Following the signs for baggage claim, Charlotte dodged and weaved through suitcases and bodies that pressed in every direction. Near the carousel, a stylish woman cut through the chaos, waving energetically.

Charlotte broke into a smile, quickened her pace, and flew into her aunt's arms.

"Ahhhh!" Aunt Becky squeezed her, then cupped her goddaughter's face. "Look at you, girl. You are gorgeous."

Always fashionable, her aunt wore a tailored ivory dress with low heels and exquisite gold jewelry.

"Thanks."

"How are you? How was your flight? Did you check a bag?"

Charlotte nodded.

"Okay, which one is yours?"

They found her bag, marked with a bright neon ribbon tied to the handle to make it easy to recognize, and piled into a waiting cab.

Looking out the cab window, the sky greeted her with a blinding blue color, brighter than anything back home, with big puffy cotton-ball clouds. Tall palm trees whizzed past the windows as they merged onto the freeway, and Charlotte craned her neck as the buildings stretched higher into the sky. Oak Falls' tallest structure was its city hall. It didn't compare in the slightest.

She pressed her face against the glass as the city unfolded before her, recognizing a few buildings from the movie *L.A. Story*. Highways stacked and split as ramps spiraled in different directions. The movies and pictures she'd seen couldn't have prepared her for this metropolis.

Charlotte laughed. Oak Falls had two major highways. That was it. The driver slid onto the 405 highway.

"We're just about into Hollywood now," Aunt Becky said.

Charlotte didn't blink.

Soon they pulled up to the curb in front of a gated apartment building. It was a beautiful, storied historic building with ivy growing up the walls, landscaped bushes and flowers decorating the courtyard, and of course a few palm trees lining the street.

"Welcome to your new home for the next six weeks," Aunt Becky said as she paid the driver.

"You live here?" Charlotte slung her bag over her shoulder, going across the little courtyard and through the oak front doors. The elegant lobby was decorated with creams and ivories. The red tiled floor echoed her aunt's heel sounds as they approached the elevator. They rose up to the fourth floor and went down a narrow hallway to door 401C.

Aunt Becky ushered Charlotte inside. "Whoa."

It was like heaven or her vision of it.

Sunlight washed the white apartment in a warm, fuzzy glow. The fresh scent of hydrangeas drifted from the glass dining table. The fluffy couch tickled Charlotte's fingertips as she took in the modern art hanging on the walls. What impressed her the most was the enormous entertainment center housing a large television and the latest stereo system.

Her aunt was a photographer, a well-off one by the looks of her apartment. Many of her photographs had been featured on the covers of major magazines. She photographed celebrities, musicians, models, fashion shows, concerts, and charity events. She had the gift to make anyone look glamorous. According to what her mom told her, Aunt Becky was quite in demand.

"This is like something out of a magazine. It's so modern."

Aunt Becky threw her head back with an angelic laugh and set down her purse on the entry table. "I'll show you where you can put your things."

Down the short hall to the left was a room that held a pristine bed with a velvety pink seashell headboard and white sheets. It was framed by billowy lace curtains. On the side table sat a phone.

Her own phone. Charlotte squealed.

"This'll be your room. Feel free to use the dresser and the closet for your clothes. The bathroom is out in the hall on your left, and my room is opposite you. Make this place your home."

Charlotte dumped her luggage on the floor and went back into the living room. Aunt Becky offered her a Coke and made sandwiches while they gossiped and caught up. Charlotte was grateful her aunt found time to host her, let alone spend time with her. She slumped a little. Aunt Becky had time for her. Her own mother didn't.

"So is your mom still not seeing anyone?"

"She's still very single."

"A woman that gorgeous needs to find herself a man."

"I could say the same thing about you," Charlotte teased.

"Pfft. I'm still having too much fun to settle down."

Charlotte shook her head as she stuffed her mouth.

While they talked about Aunt Becky's work, Charlotte had to pull and prod her aunt into dropping a few famous names she'd photographed. It was taboo to brag about clients in the industry, and her aunt was a classy lady who revered her job. So the few names Charlotte was given, she relished.

"No way. You've met Johnny Depp?" Charlotte squished her cheeks. "What was he like? Was he nice? Isn't he drop-dead gorgeous?"

Aunt Becky sipped from her glass. "Yes, he is handsome and very nice. Shy boy."

Charlotte collapsed dramatically on the pillowy couch. "Oh, Aunt Becky."

"He's a bit young for me." Aunt Becky chuckled and set down her cup on the glass coffee table. "But I do see his appeal. It's all in his eyes. Now, we have some plans to discuss, missy."

Charlotte shot forward, her toes squishing into the creamy rug.

"I have a few shoots I couldn't get out of over the next few days. I hope you aren't too disappointed."

"That's all right. Out here, I have sort of a reluctant big brother from our time growing up in Oak Falls. Matt. He'll show me some sights." Time to resume her mission to win him over. Heck, it never stopped.

"Oh, good. But I have some ideas for us over this summer." She squeezed the teenager's hand. "I'm so happy you're here. We're going to have so much fun. In the meantime, if you want to freshen up, go ahead. Then tonight, I'm going to take you to one of my favorite restaurants. It's casual attire. And they prepare the most mouthwatering sushi."

Charlotte grimaced. "Do they . . . um . . . make other things? And cook them?"

"Not a fan? They have other options you can try. Okay, scoot. Go get ready."

Charlotte pinched herself to make sure this wasn't a dream.

Saturday morning. First official day in California. From the balcony of her castle, the city looked like a distant kingdom. The sunrise warmed everything it touched. Nestled amongst trees were apartments and houses, and beyond that were endless buildings. It was noisy with car horns and engines roaring.

Charlotte grinned.

Back home, infinite trees with the occasional white steeple peeked through a sea of green. A dog barking and birds singing was her home's bland tune. Charlotte heaved a sigh.

First on her agenda was to learn about the neighborhood. She walked several blocks, memorizing street names and landmarks. Post office, mini-mart, city bus stop. Everyone was in a constant rush. Cars cluttered the streets. The energy in the air buzzed. She didn't know quite how to describe it. Downtown Oak Falls was sleepy. Pedestrians strolled with nowhere to be, and drivers idled as they waved at passersby.

She purchased a few postcards, headed back to the ritzy apartment, and spent time memorizing the interview questions Jason had written, determined to be ready.

Twelve thirty.

Finally.

It was time.

Changing into a floral-print summer dress with spaghetti straps, she crammed her feet into her Converse shoes. With a chunky purse slung over her shoulder, she inspected her outfit in the mirror. Playful yet professional with a beachy vibe. First impressions were everything.

Just as Aunt Becky advised, Charlotte ordered a cab to the Santa Monica Pier. Dropped off at the entrance, she passed underneath the towering archway with the crowd.

Banners along the Santa Monica Pier billed the weekend's run of shows as a kickoff to next month's concert series. Caravan was listed among the artists.

Charlotte was swept up in the foot traffic but found an opportunity to break away. It was all a bit overwhelming. In the respite near the railing, she was able to drink it all in at her own pace. Seagulls screamed over the murmur of the crowd and jazz music. Leaning over the pier, she felt the spray of the crashing waves. Surfers and sunbathers dotted the beach, while sailboats and yachts drifted up and down on the rocky waves.

She snapped a few pictures, then turned back to the crowd. "Get your guts up, Charlotte." And with that, she dove back into the mob of people.

Squeezing out of the traffic, she stopped under a shaded vendor to buy more postcards. The scent of fried fish tickled her nostrils, and her stomach grumbled. Thinking it might be time for a late lunch, she found refuge in The Albright, a cheery seafood restaurant, and ordered their fish and chips.

Armed with a full stomach and chewing gum, because no one wants fish breath during an interview, Charlotte nudged her way toward the music. Many people had set up lawn chairs facing a raised platform with the ocean as a backdrop. Onlookers stood and watched the musicians, and some danced. This was more her speed.

When the music ended, Charlotte popped a bubble and joined in on the applause. The sky's clarity and brightness amazed her.

Someone over the microphone introduced Caravan, and she snapped back to attention. The crowd cheered at the mere mention of the band's name. She stood on her tiptoes and strained her neck. The band trickled onto the covered stage.

Her eyes homed in on the man who went to the right side of the platform. The man with a guitar slung around his shoulders.

It was him.

It was Jesse Holt.

He pressed a pedal on the ground and turned to the drummer. A lively beat pounded on the bass drum as Danny told the audience to clap. High-spirited repetitive beats on the toms from the drummer led into Jesse Holt playing the intro to "Here We Go." The crowd screamed at the rocky and familiar tune.

Charlotte stood mesmerized. They owned the stage. The music was loud and energetic. People danced and sang along with the nostalgic lyrics.

Danny Racer, older than the pictures she had familiarized herself with, hit all the notes with practiced precision. His voice was crisp and clean. How he was not out of breath from running back and forth and jumping around the stage was a mystery to her. He still had the *it* quality.

Impressive as he was, Charlotte's gaze circled back to the guitarist.

Jesse Holt smiled at individual members of the crowd and threw his picks their way. When it was time for his solo, his skills were even better than on the album. He deviated a little from the recorded solos she had already memorized over the last week. He added extra flourish or an insane lick. It was crazy to admit it, but they sounded better live than on their album. All Charlotte could do was stare at him.

About two songs in, Charlotte snapped out of her trance. She needed to find Matt. It was getting easier to worm her way through the crowd.

On the side of the stage, a few crewmen wearing lanyards stood behind a rope, barring access. A canvas drop cloth blocked off the backstage area. Straining to find Matt among the crewmen, she gave up and stepped over the rope. "Excuse me. Hi there, I'm looking for Matt Kendrick. Have you seen him?"

"You shouldn't be over here," one of them said as he displayed his arms out.

A young-looking man with bronze skin and blond hair pulled back into a ponytail approached her. He smoked a cigarette and wore a fitted T-shirt and faded jeans. "What do you want?"

"Matt! It's me, Charlotte. Jason told you to expect me."

He adjusted his sunglasses and stamped out his cigarette. "Right."

"You've gotten taller and darker. A lot darker than your brother. I bet this West Coast sun is to blame," she said, gesturing to the sunshine beating down. "You've grown your hair long. It suits you, I guess. I haven't seen it down yet. Never thought about you with long hair, but I guess that's how it is out here. I mean, Brad Pitt, Johnny Depp, they all have long hair now. What I mean is you look like someone who lives in California."

"You done talking?"

Charlotte wrinkled her nose as she gave him a big smile. "Yep."

He pulled a lanyard out of his back pocket and let it drop from his hand. A backstage pass. "Gonna be honest, I didn't think you'd show up."

Charlotte raised an eyebrow and flashed her white teeth. "Let's be honest, you didn't want me to show up."

"You got that right. Here. Wear this."

"Thanks."

The lanyard hung around her neck.

Jason had updated her about his cousin before she left. Matt Kendrick had worked as a local roadie in the California area since he was eighteen. Around twenty-two now, Matt was something of a well-rounded roadie. He was knowledgeable about the back end of shows and concerts. Efficient in loading and unloading trucks, lighting, sound, and grip work, he could do it all. And because of his good work ethic, he was respected by many musicians in the area.

Matt liked to keep busy and, according to Jason, was a bit of an eccentric. Which, in Jason's opinion, you had to be if you were a roadie. It's a lot of hard work.

"Come with me." He dipped behind the canvas, not even waiting for her.

Charlotte followed. "Thanks for letting me tag along. Jason must have something pretty big over you for you to agree to do this."

"You could say that. Babysitting a teen-crazed fan is not something I ever agreed to do. So you tell my sniveling cousin we're even."

Charlotte's eyes narrowed. "I'm not some teen-crazed fan."

"Right, you're here to write an article for your school paper. Please."

"It's true."

It was Matt's turn to narrow his eyes as he lowered his sunglasses just enough to glare at her over the top. "You and Jase are up to something. Lucky for you, I don't care enough to find out. As long as it doesn't affect my job."

"It won't."

He adjusted his sunglasses before approaching a bear-like man in his mid-to-late fifties. This large imposing grizzly bounced his stocky leg to the time of the music. He exposed a toothy grin as he motioned to another colleague. That grin and his Hawaiian shirt were the only disarming qualities in his intimidating appearance.

"Hey, J. J."

The bear named J. J. stuck his paw out, and they shook. "Hey, what's going on, Matty?" His hand swallowed the roadie's hand.

Matt made introductions. "This is Charlotte Reynolds. I believe you were expecting her."

J. J. shook her hand. "Hi, Charlotte. How's it hanging?"

"Just fine, thanks." Straightening her back, she tried to imitate her aunt: a mix of grace, class, and a healthy amount of professionalism. This was Mr. Jeremy Jackson, otherwise known as J. J., the manager of Caravan. Since the creation of the band, he had been their manager. One of the articles at the library credited his tireless work in driving the band's success. If she wasn't careful, he could stand between her and meeting her supposed father. "Thank you for allowing me to interview the band."

"No sweat." He waved the favor away. "Matt's a good guy."

Charlotte elbowed the roadie. "We go way back."

Matt made a face and took a few steps further away.

J. J. wiped the perspiration from his forehead, then readjusted the cap on his head. "Well, any friend of Matt's is a friend of mine. I understand you have a paper you're writing."

"Yes. I'm with Harrison High, and there was some talk about getting rid of the band and the fine arts departments because of funding issues. My teacher thought it'd be a cool idea to feature a band in an article for the school board, along with a petition."

J. J. laughed. "And you chose these guys?"

"My teacher is a major fan."

"If he wants, I can get him a couple of tickets."

"She'd like that," she politely corrected.

She and Jason had thought the plan through. If something like this happened and they needed a tangible teacher, Charlotte could convince Aunt Becky to play the part. Her aunt was always down for adventure, but as of right now, she was on a need-to-know basis.

"Bring her around some time."

"Will do."

"It's nice to see these old guys can still reach young kids like you. Every year we see more and more generations come out to our shows. This crowd here are parents who grew up with the band. Now they're bringing their kids."

"That proves their relatability and talent."

"They've done a few of these types of interviews before with students. They jump at the chance to help kids learn music. I think they just love talking about themselves." He chuckled. "So when's your article going to be published? In the school paper or something?"

"Um . . . well." They hadn't thought of every answer. "Uh—probably the end of summer or the start of the school year. I'll be sure to send you a copy."

"Very cool." He slapped his hands together. "Okay, so here's what's going to happen. You'll have a chance to interview the band here at the Pier. I'll make introductions today when they're done, you can ask a few questions, but typically, it's best if you come before the shows to ask your questions. Especially for the evening gigs. These old timers like to go back home to their families afterward."

"Got it."

"When you're all done, I'll give you two tickets for one of their July concerts at the Hollywood Bowl."

Her round eyes widened. "What?"

The Hollywood Bowl was a historic outdoor amphitheater, famous for its natural acoustics and iconic arched band shell. Legends like The Beatles and The Beach Boys had played there.

"I like to do that for the students."

Charlotte took his hand and shook it energetically. "Mr. Jackson, thank you. Thank you, so much."

One of Caravan's songs started.

"This is their last song," J. J. said.

They waited by the side of the stage a few feet from the stairs. It was a short show. Charlotte had counted six songs.

Matt sighed loudly behind her while looking at his watch, making his resentment known.

Danny Racer held his last note, then shouted, "Thank you! We love you!"

The crowd roared, and J. J. clapped as if he, too, was an avid fan. The crowd went nuts as the group gathered together and took a collective bow.

Her heart pounded, sweat coated her palms, and those pesky butterflies darn near flittered up and out of her mouth.

The band walked across the stage and descended the steps. Jesse Holt still had his guitar around his neck until he reached the bottom and handed it off to his technician. Each member gulped bottled water passed to them and mopped their brows as the bright sun blazed overhead.

"Nice show guys," their manager called out. "Hey, wait a minute. I have someone I want you to meet."

Charlotte's knees wobbled, and her fingers shook. All last week this had been a dream and a wish. Now it was coming true. It wasn't exciting. It was nauseating.

She gripped the notebook with her questions, inwardly thanking Jason for writing them down. Over and over, she told herself to keep it together and act like her aunt. Her quivering jaw tried to show confidence, but she was sure they saw through her act. The only thing going for her was the show of holding her shoulders back. She hoped it would be enough to pass as a professional asking questions and not some teen-crazed fan.

Several of the band members recognized Matt, greeting him with warm smiles and handshakes. How did he stand it, knowing all these celebrities?

Oh, no. She still had gum in her mouth. With her tongue, she pushed it to the side and reminded herself not to look at Jesse, not even once, or she'd stare at him the whole time.

"This is Matt's friend, Charlotte Reynolds with Harrison High. She's writing an article for her school, and I don't know why, but her subject is you guys." The band chuckled. "I wanted to make introductions before she starts asking you all a bunch of questions. We're setting up interview times for her with you all before a few of the shows at the Pier. Be on your best behavior."

Charlotte forced herself to interject, "I want our school to keep the musical arts program. This interview would be a great way to do that."

They all straightened and started nodding their heads in agreement.

Jason was so smart.

Their manager glanced at his watch. "They only have a few minutes. But I'll send you home with a list of their shows and times." Then he turned and left her with the group.

There she was standing with six rock stars. All of them towered over her.

Behind her, Matt cleared his throat, which forced her to smile. Be professional. Inside her notebook, the questions were blurry and barely visible. Her mind went blank. Mayday. Mayday.

She swallowed her nausea and looked up at the lead singer, Danny. He was the closest to her. Those magazine pictures didn't do him justice. His feathered hair was so perfectly out of place. His golden eyes sparkled in the sunlight. "You've got pretty eyes."

Why did she say that? Why the heck did she just say that? So much for being professional.

"Thank you, Charlotte." His smile was mesmerizing.

Focusing on the paper was hard when all she could think about was that he said her name. Get it together. Blundering on, she tried to salvage her first impression despite feeling like an idiot. "Well . . . uh, I'll start with an easy one. Who came up with the name Caravan and what does it mean?"

Roy, she recognized as the drummer, spoke up first in a loud, brash voice. "Mike thought of the name, and he'll tell you all about it right now."

They all snickered.

Mike, the keyboard player and founding member of the group, smirked. "It's a vehicle you can live in while traveling."

They all snickered again.

Charlotte giggled at his playful response. "I'm well aware of that. But what made you think of it for the band name?"

"His brain," Reggie, the bass player, chimed in. "It was hard for such a tiny brain."

He was smacked in the head by another member.

Mike adjusted his glasses. "It seemed like a good idea at the time. I think it started as a placeholder and then kind of stuck."

"We couldn't think of a better one," Roy bellowed.

"It's sad really," Reggie interjected.

Charlotte laughed nervously and eyed her questions. Which one should she ask next? They were all so serious for a first meeting. It never occurred to her to pick and choose certain ones. Clearing her throat, she went off script. "Um, and when did you guys start? I mean, how did you guys start?"

Going off script—bad idea.

The rhythm guitarist placed a hand on his chest. His name was Scott, and he was Mike's brother. "My brother and I started in our parent's basement when we were teenagers. We wanted to play rock 'n' roll like a lot of our friends. We were influenced by Jimi Hendrix and The Beatles and other groups at that time."

Danny interjected with his velvety smooth-like-butter voice. "I went to school with these two dunderheads, and they had to drag me into their little setup. We started writing tunes, and the rest is history. It all kind of fell into place."

Charlotte caught herself staring at him. Not looking even once at Jesse Holt had been a bad idea. Gushing over the singer just proved Matt's theory—she was a crazy fan.

Knowing her first impression was blown, she ended the interview. "That's it for now. Thank you so much for your time."

They all shook her hand and thanked her. Jesse immediately went to his technician who was tuning his guitars for the evening show.

She crimped her lips together as they dispersed. A total bust. Glancing back, she felt the heat of Matt's fiery gaze behind his sunglasses. He'd take her lanyard away.

Determined to prove she wasn't a stupid crazed-fan teenager, Charlotte gripped her backstage pass and flagged down the keyboardist. "Mr. Tennet."

"Ooof, call me Mike."

"All right, Mike. Um . . . how influential was playing an instrument to you growing up?"

He shifted his weight and rubbed his chin as the memories were recalled. "Extremely influential and very important. Music helped things make sense to me. School was tough, but when I started playing, it clicked in my head. It was almost mathematical but in a way I could understand. It was my saving grace at school."

"Thank you." She offered a firm handshake.

He grinned and said goodbye. His smile said it all. Approval. She did it.

What did he say? She had to write it down. Even though she wasn't writing this article, his answer was good, and she wanted to remember every single moment of this trip. Besides, Jason would kill her if she didn't write their answers to his questions. She rummaged in her purse for a pen.

"That was the most painful thing I've ever had to witness," Matt said when he came beside her.

"Oh, shut up." Charlotte hastily jotted down his answer.

"I don't want any part of this."

"I saved it in the end." She tossed her notebook into her bag. "Like you've never tripped over your words? Oh, that's right, you hardly ever say any."

A wide smile spread across her face, and she placed her hands on her hips.

"Excuse me, Miss Reynolds?"

Charlotte turned around. A ball hitched in her throat.

Jesse Holt.

He stood a few inches away from her.

"Hey, it was nice to meet you." His voice was velvety with a twinge of an accent. "Charlotte, was it?"

She nodded.

"What you're doing is really cool, and I'll be looking forward to reading your article." He smiled and said goodbye, and a dimple appeared on his right cheek, mirroring her own.

"Um. Bye," she croaked.

"Unbelievable," Matt said, then walked away.

Charlotte stood—unmoving. He spoke to her.

Her supposed father spoke to her.

Chapter 7

Painting the Town

Before leaving, she confirmed her interview dates with the band's manager for the next week. Then Matt escorted her out of the Pier and toward a row of taxis waiting for tourists.

"Gee, Matt, you're the best," Charlotte said in an extra cheery tone as she nudged him.

"Whatever."

"Oh, come on. It must be exciting to have celebrities know you by name?"

"Even for a teenager, that was the worst thing I've seen. You're going to mess everything up."

"Matty."

"Don't call me that."

She faced him with a big grin. "I think we're going to have the best summer of our lives."

Opening the car door, he paid the cabbie. "I gotta get back."

Charlotte rattled off the address to the driver. "Thanks, Matt."

With one nod, he left, serving up that coldness she knew all too well. The challenge had been accepted.

Over takeout that evening, Aunt Becky excitedly grilled her on what wonderful events she had been up to that day. Charlotte was careful not to divulge her true plans but relayed meeting Matt and taking in the sites at the Pier. It wasn't a total lie.

The sun hit her face, and she stirred. A sleepy Sunday morning. Adjusting to the brightness, she pried one eye open at a time, burrowing deeper into the soft, cozy bed. The alarm clock numbers glowed nine a.m., LA time. She yawned and did the math; it was about noon back home. Jason would be up by now. Hopefully. He'd sleep the summer away if he could.

Rolling over, she reached for the phone by her nightstand and yawned again as she punched in her best friend's home phone number.

"Hunter residence," Mrs. Hunter's chipper voice answered after the second ring.

Charlotte grinned and spoke quietly, "Hi, Mrs. Hunter, it's Charlotte."

"Hi, Charlotte. How is sunny California?"

"It's super cool. Is Jason home?"

"He sure is." She called for her son, and after some rustling, he came to the phone almost out of breath.

"Tell me everything. Did you meet them?" Jason walked from the kitchen back to his room, the long cord of the phone trailing behind.

"It was amazing."

"Did you see the show? Did you find Matt? Did you get to meet your father?" He whispered the last part even behind his bedroom door.

She squished into the pillow top. "They are totally amazing live. Like better than I could've ever imagined. And they don't look like old guys trying to recapture their youth, you know? They look like rock stars."

"What about Matt? Did you meet him? Was he nice to you?"

"Oh, I see us having a grand time this summer." She chuckled. "I never got to ask, what is it you have over him?"

"The less you know the better." He shuddered over the airwaves.

"That bad, huh?"

"If I told you, I'd probably have to kill you."

Charlotte stifled a laugh. "All right, I won't press it."

"So did you meet them after the show? How'd they like my questions?"

"I met their manager, Mr. Jackson. Jase, you should've seen him. He's like a grizzly bear. Only thing that kept me from running away with my tail between my legs was his smile. Otherwise, he might've chewed me up and spit me out."

"He seemed nice over the phone."

"Oh, he was super nice, but he's definitely in the right business. He looks like a don't-take-no-for-an-answer kind of manager. He introduced me to the band and set up times to interview them next."

"So you met him? You met Jesse Holt?"

"I was so nervous. At first, I kind of blew it. Made a downright fool of myself and told Danny he had pretty eyes. Right to his face."

"Weirdo."

"I know. I'm such a dork. I don't know what came over me. I've never met any major celebrities. The only celebrity I've ever met was Miss South Carolina when Mayor Johnson got her to be in our float parade, but she isn't even in the same league as these guys."

"I don't understand you girls."

"Shut up."

"But you pulled it together?"

"Yeah. They were being funny and wouldn't quite answer my questions, and it was a bit confusing. Looking back at it, I think they could tell I was nervous and tried to break the ice by cracking jokes. Oh, and you'll never guess what happened next. As they were leaving, Jesse personally told me he can't wait to read my article."

"That's cool."

"Makes me a little sorry I'm not writing a real article."

"You could write one just to give them something. It doesn't have to be perfect or anything."

"Jason, I can write school essays, but I don't know how to write an article."

"I can help."

"No, I can't have you do that. I'd be making you cookies for the rest of my natural-born life. I'll figure something out."

"Make sure you're writing down all their answers. I want to read everything when you come back home."

"Any major news while I've been gone?"

"You've been gone a day and a half."

She shrugged. "I know."

"Guess who has a job shelving movies?"

Charlotte rang out a laugh. "I don't envy you. But the money'll be nice."

"That's what I said. Oh, the ice cream shop rolled out their new summer flavors."

"The boysenberry one?"

"You got it."

"Oh, man, I can't wait to get me some when I get back."

"Kim did give me an update on the whole Britney thing. I guess when she heard you flew out to California, she was jealous. Kim said she didn't admit it, but she could tell."

"Really?"

"I think you have a leg up on Britney's summer plans, which are just hanging around this small town."

Charlotte toyed with her hair between her fingers. "While I like the thought of her being jealous, I don't need her to make my life worse when I come back."

"Don't worry about future what-ifs. Just worry about doing all sorts of fun things in between the concerts and interviews. And if Britney just so happens to hear about it, well that'd be icing on the cake."

Aunt Becky whisked into the room with a fashionable outfit and full face of makeup perfection. "Good morning, my dear. Who are you talking to?"

"My friend, Jason."

"Right. Well, you tell Jason goodbye. We have plans to make and breakfast to eat." She floated out of the room.

Charlotte swung her legs over the side of the bed. "That's my cue to leave, Jase."

"Keep me updated."

"Oh, hey. Can I get Matt's phone number?"

Jason called out to his mom who relayed the number to him, and he relayed it to Charlotte.

"Got it. Thanks. And thanks for everything."

"Bye, Lotty."

Changing into a short red skirt and a white sheer top with a black spaghetti strap camisole underneath, she joined her aunt in the kitchen.

Aunt Becky had made them eggs and toast. "Who was it you were talking to? Who is he? What's he like?"

"It's Jason, my best friend. I told you about him. We've known each other since we were like five."

"And do you usually call him early in the morning?" She grinned.

Charlotte shoveled eggs into her mouth. "Aunt Becky, it's almost lunchtime there."

"Is he cute?"

"I guess so. He was telling me about some things back home."

Aunt Becky wasn't going to give up on her speculations but conceded for now. "And anything interesting happen?"

"The ice cream parlor got three new flavors for the summer."

Aunt Becky rapped her fingers on the counter. "We need to work on your definition of juicy gossip. So. On to more exciting news. What are some of the sites you want to see this summer?"

Charlotte leaned in with a twinkle in her eye. "I want to see everything. I'm in Los Angeles, city of the stars. I want to experience everything."

Aunt Becky clapped her hands together and exclaimed. "This'll be great. I have so many plans for us. Plays, concerts, shopping, manicures, facials. The works."

"Don't forget Disneyland and the beach."

Aunt Becky produced two tickets to the famous theme park and Charlotte screamed. "We're going to have so much fun."

The day flew by in a blur of rides and sugar: spinning teacups, fast tracks, sticky fingers from churros and cotton candy. Music drifted through the park along with laughter and screams of joy. They waited in lines as the crowds around them buzzed with excitement. Parents hoisted their kids onto their hips, and dads pointed out the castles and princesses.

Just when Charlotte thought Sunday couldn't be more perfect, the next day promised even more. As anxious as she was to meet and learn more about her father, she couldn't wait to explore Hollywood.

They got manicures and pedicures before they went to some of her aunt's favorite boutiques, buying little souvenirs, jewelry, and perfume. Since Aunt Becky didn't live too far from Hollywood, they dropped everything off at the apartment before walking to a bistro for lunch.

Next, they went to Grauman's Chinese Theatre to admire the Hollywood Walk of Fame. For years, this sidewalk had honored celebrities by sealing their handprints and footprints in cement. It was packed with tourists and their cameras like sardines crammed into a tin can. They wormed their way through the sea of people.

A dad carried his daughter on his shoulders, poking her sides to make her laugh. Another clutched his son tight against his chest, shielding him from the chaos. Charlotte felt the familiar ache in her chest. It was brief, then gone almost as soon as it came.

Charlotte froze at seeing Marilyn Monroe's prints and signature forever in cement.

"Aunt Becky! Take a picture of me."

"Talk about memories. Your mom used to place her hands in Marilyn Monroe's handprints. I liked Elizabeth Taylor."

"You two came here often?"

"Oh my, yes. We walked these streets all the time every summer she came out to visit."

Charlotte kneeled and placed her hands in the blond bombshell's handprints, and her aunt snapped a picture. Once developed, she'd have to send that one to her mom.

"What else did you all do around here?"

"We'd hang out at the malls and scope out the cute boys. Sometimes we'd pick a few up and sneak into a movie. And never watch the movie." Aunt Becky elbowed her goddaughter with a sly grin.

"My mom did that?" Charlotte snapped another photo of the circular Capitol Records Building and continued down the boulevard toward the Strip. "What else?"

Aunt Becky gave a mischievous smile and stuck out her thumb as a truck passed by.

"What are you doing?" Charlotte exclaimed as she seized her aunt's arm.

The truck pulled over to the curb, and the bearded man leaned over. "Do you need a ride, ma'am?"

"Ma'am?!" Aunt Becky sounded flabbergasted.

"No," Charlotte interjected. "Thank you, we're good."

The man nodded, then pulled back onto the road.

"What on earth were you trying to do?" Charlotte asked.

Aunt Becky burst into a fit of laughter. "I haven't done that in years."

"You hitchhiked?"

"All the time, honey." They walked toward Melrose Avenue. "We used to hitchhike all up and down the coast."

"My mom? Hitchhiked?"

"You haven't heard the half of it. And just so you know, I wouldn't have actually put us in that guy's truck back there. Your mom would've had my head. But the '70s were just a different time."

They stopped in front of the Paramount Pictures gates.

Charlotte posed with extra flourish, and her aunt snapped the photo.

They toured the Hollywood Forever Cemetery. It was kind of a depressing experience viewing the gravestones of Hollywood's elites. She was glad when they left.

When exiting the cemetery, the famous Hollywood Sign, perched on a faraway hillside, came into view. "Oh, Aunt Becky we have to go up and see it."

"My dear, we can see anything you want over the next few weeks, but right now my feet feel like they are going to fall off. I think we should call it a day."

Despite wanting to see more, Charlotte realized the aching of her own feet and was suddenly tired just thinking about their walk home. Charlotte, forced to end their glorious day, took a final photo of the Hollywood Sign.

Arriving back at the apartment, they shuffled their feet inside, dropping purses with a clunk. Sinking into the fluffy couch, Charlotte winced at wiggling her toes. It had been such a good day.

"We must have walked a thousand miles," Aunt Becky hissed with each step. "I think we should call in a pizza for tonight. I don't want to go out, do you?" Aunt Becky sifted through her mail.

Charlotte welcomed a night in, tempted by a bubble bath. "Looks like you have a message." A red light flickered on the answering machine.

A male voice spoke on the recording, reminding Aunt Becky of a photo shoot in the morning. Locations and times were listed off through the speaker. "Oh, no. I thought that was next week." Aunt Becky flipped through her calendar book, and sure enough, the photo shoot was slated for the next day. "How could I have gotten this mixed up?"

Charlotte gave a reassuring grin. "It's all right, Aunt Becky. It'll be fine."

"It means the next few days are going to be tied up."

"That's fine."

"Abandoning you? This was supposed to be our fun vacation."

She propped her arms on the back of the couch, "You won't be abandoning me. I'm a pro at finding things to do by myself. I don't want you to miss an appointment because of me. Really. It's all right."

"I hate to leave you all alone."

"It won't be a problem. I can make Matt hang out with me."

Aunt Becky chuckled. "Let me know if you ever get him to crack a smile."

Charlotte buried her head in her arms at the daunting task.

The night ended with pizza, laughter, and then a honeysuckle-scented bubble bath that eased her sore muscles. When was the last time she'd had a night like that with her mom?

As she popped a few bubbles on her arm, her mind replayed what her aunt had revealed about her mom. They used to hitchhike and pick up boys. How little did she know about her mom?

Chapter 8

Tower Records

Charlotte spent the next two days sleeping late and wandering the neighborhood in the afternoons while Aunt Becky worked. Their evenings were easy and quiet but waiting for the next meeting with Caravan wasn't.

The band returned to the Pier for their Friday evening show, and Charlotte had already memorized the questions she would ask. She was determined to have a successful interview.

With hours to kill on show day, Charlotte had an idea and picked up the phone.

"Hello?" A disgruntled, sleepy voice answered the phone.

"Hi, Matt. It's me, Charlotte."

An audibly annoyed sigh came from the other end. "I thought you quit."

"I interview them tonight. Anyway, I wanted to buy you breakfast or lunch in exchange for showing me your favorite spots around town?" She crossed her fingers during the long silence.

"Fine. Where you at?"

Charlotte gave her address, then quickly got dressed in some denim shorts and a white button-down blouse she tied into a knot at the bottom. Putting on her Converse and hooking some hoop earrings in her ears, she raced outside to wait for him.

A red Toyota Camry pulled up to the curb, and she hopped in.

Dressed in baggy jean shorts and a Billabong T-shirt, he had pulled his long hair low into a ponytail. With these details and his sunglasses, he reminded her of a surfer—one that was hungover.

"Are you a late sleeper?"

"When I work until two in the morning." He put the car in drive and pulled out. "Where do you want to go?"

"Is there a good music store around here?"

"Yeah." After a short drive, he turned into a building on the Sunset Strip with a big yellow sign and bold letters saying Tower Records. "If you need music, this is the place to go."

As they stepped out of the car, Charlotte snapped a picture of the yellow awning. Nearby, a group of teens lounged on their hoods, smoking and talking.

The cold AC from the music store gave her instant goosebumps. A powerful scent wrinkled her nostrils, the kind of smell found only in the best record shops—must and cardboard. She grinned. There were rows upon rows of music. A song blasted over the speakers as many teens laughed and danced to the music.

As she and Matt walked through the rows of music, her fingertips brushed over the different sections, and she paused at the country section. She smiled thinking of Olivia and her ambitions of being a country singer. Country music was a popular choice for them when driving around town on hot summer days. One particularly memorable ride was when they blasted all kinds of revenge songs after Olivia's boyfriend broke up with her. Clay Walker's "What's It to You" was on repeat.

Charlotte passed by another section. Opera. Making a face, she moved on to yet another section. "So, Matt. What is your favorite music to listen to?"

"Heavy metal, I guess. Some stuff from the '80s. And some blues and R & B."

He showed her a few records and CDs of particular bands.

As they thumbed through albums, she tried a few conversation starters. "Why were you up till two in the morning?"

"Tearing down and loading up equipment."

With an inquisitive playful look, she leaned toward him. "You see, this is where you tell a curious mind the *for whom* part."

Rolling his eyes, he said, "There was a function going on last night. Several artists played their own sets and then collaborated at the end."

"Sounds interesting. Which ones?"

"Paul Rodgers, Jeff Beck, and a few others."

"Jeff Beck? You met Jeff Beck?"

"No. I just set up the rigging."

His flippant attitude toward working so close to such legends was baffling. In the alternative rock section situated under a flickering fluorescent light, she squealed at finding Caravan's debut album in CD form. She'd purchase it and ask the band to sign it for Jason.

"You really like them?" His voice sounded judgmental.

"You don't?" Charlotte was hurt. His attitude was that if he didn't approve of them, then it was a big deal.

"No, I do. They've got some great music. I didn't expect a kid like you to dig their stuff."

"I'm not much younger than you."

"You really know their music? With this whole school thing you're doing?"

"Yep. I own all their albums and have heard several of their songs on the radio." Moving to the H section, she let out an audible gasp. In her hands, was a solo album by Jesse Holt. "No way. He did a solo album? Have you heard it?"

"Didn't even know he had one."

She studied the CD cover. It was called *Moonlight* and was produced in 1986. New music. This was fantastic. They wandered the record store a little longer before she made her purchases. When going outside, they were hit with rays of the sun. Charlotte tilted her head back and threw her arms out as if soaking in every beam of light available. The California sun was deliciously warm and inviting.

"You're kinda weird."

Charlotte squinted and followed him toward the car. "Thanks!"

"So what instrument do you play?"

"I don't play an instrument."

Matt pulled down his shades. "You don't play an instrument, yet you're writing an article campaigning to keep music in your school."

Charlotte gulped. She walked right into that one. "I don't have to play an instrument to know its significance."

He eyed her for a moment before unlocking the car. "You and Jason are up to something."

Charlotte laughed and slid into the passenger seat. "I never knew you to be so paranoid."

"Least you're not a crazed fan. I wasn't so sure the other day."

The engine roared to life.

"I'm glad you've come to that conclusion."

"I told you I don't need you ruining my reputation."

"Have a little faith in me."

The car reversed and pulled out of the parking lot. Charlotte straightened. There it was. Both of her eyes were glued to the famous club talked about all the time on MTV. Pointing urgently out the window, she screeched, "That's The Viper Room!"

She snapped a hasty picture, knowing it'd turn out blurry. Who cares? It was The Viper Room.

"Yep."

She hoped to catch a glimpse of Johnny Depp exiting the famous bar, knowing full well he wouldn't. "Have you been inside? Have you met Johnny Depp? What's it like in there? Is it the best place you've ever been?"

"Just when I think I got you pegged, you go and act like an obsessive fangirl."

She pouted her lips. "You gotta give me this. It's Johnny Depp. You know. *Edward Scissorhands. 21 Jump Street.* I mean, he's gorgeous."

"Just because he owns The Viper Room doesn't mean he's always there. And yes, I've been inside."

Like a puppy dog, all wide-eyed and playful, she leaned on the armrest, desperate to hear more.

He exhaled. "It's dark, edgy. Decent drinks. It's not all it's hyped up to be."

"Was he in there when you were there?"

"I saw him once."

She squealed, seizing and squeezing his arm. "You saw him?"

"For a moment, yes. I take it back. You are a psycho fan."

"Just for him." She collapsed back into her seat. "And maybe Bon Jovi a close second."

The Toyota pulled into a '50s-themed diner called Johnny Rockets.

"I saw this the other day with my aunt." She snapped her camera.

"They've got good burgers."

"I could eat two." Her stomach growled as they went inside. The place was loud as old music played and people chatted. Clinking silverware and plates echoed from the kitchen. A dish clattered to the floor somewhere as they found a booth.

"Now, remember I'm buying. Ah . . . I insist." She pointed her finger with emphasis at him when he was about to protest.

Their waitress came by, and Matt quickly gave his order, then excused himself to go to the restroom. Charlotte ordered two hamburgers for herself and a side of fries with a chocolate shake and a Coke.

When Matt returned, she asked, "So why have you always been a bit of a grouch?"

He made a face.

"I'm just kidding. I know that's who you are. You can't help it," she teased. "Do you like what you do? Of course you do, otherwise you'd be doing something else. Hasn't it been four years since you moved away from Oak Falls?" She zipped her fingers across her lips and waited for him to speak.

"I left right after graduation. Wanted to get out of that town as quick as possible."

"I'm beginning to think you don't like us." Charlotte leaned on the table with a grin. "Did you just want something different?"

"Yep. People out here aren't nosey like back home. They gossip, but not everyone knows me or my family or the fact that I broke the tree swing over Miller's pond."

"I remember that. No one let you live that down for years."

Their waitress dropped off their food, and his eyes widened at the two hamburgers placed in front of her. "Whoa, you weren't kidding."

"I'm starving."

"Are you planning on eating all that?"

"Yeah. Why?"

"Most girls out here don't eat even one burger. Well, the ones I meet anyway."

"What do they eat?"

"Mostly salads."

Charlotte stopped mid-bite, her mouth open. "Oh." Starting to lower the burger but then thinking better of it, she took a huge bite. "Well, I like food," she said with a mouth full of burger.

There was a slightly impressed look on his face. "I guess so."

"I'd love to find a good pie place around here. I have a bit of a sweet tooth."

"Marie Callender's is known for their pies. The Apple Pan and Julian Pies are pretty good too."

"Maybe Aunt Becky and I'll go to one of them while I'm here. Or all three."

He shook his head, then bit into his burger.

Charlotte spent the rest of the time interrogating him about other nightclubs he'd been to. He fessed up to a few jam nights at the Whiskey a Go Go and the Rainbow with a few of his friends. There were a handful of other famous bars or clubs he'd been to that many musicians and celebrities frequented over the years.

Then she moved onto the details of his job, pressing him about which bands were awful and which ones were nice. Like her aunt, he was hesitant to name drop, but he gave her a few breadcrumbs.

"What about Caravan? Are they nice? You can give it to me straight." A fry coated in milkshake popped into her mouth.

"They are cool. I've worked with them a couple of times. Always super chill dudes."

Charlotte was glad. It'd be terrible if they were real jerks behind closed doors. "And what about Jesse Holt? Is he a pretty cool guy?"

Matt shrugged as he drank his Coke. "Yeah. He's all right. Says hi and thanks to us roadies."

She sipped her Coke. "Are you working all their shows this summer, including the one at the Pier?"

"Just the one at the Pier, so I get to hear your next interview with the band. Lucky me." He read the time on his wristwatch. "I need to get back."

She paid the bill, and he took her home.

Before walking inside the apartment, she leaned down to the open car window. "Thanks, Matt. You're pretty special, despite what Jason says."

"Hey, I have some stories about him that'll curl your hair. Ask him about the time he set fire to Mrs. Bennett's boat house."

"Oooh, I'd love to hear more. See ya tonight." She stepped back as he drove off.

Inside the apartment, the answering machine light flashed. Her aunt's voice came over the machine:

"Hi, Charlotte. I hope you're having a great time, but not *too* great since I'm not there. I am going to be a little late. I didn't think you'd be staying in for dinner, so I left some cash in my takeout drawer for you to use down at the Pier. I promise to make this up to you. Can't wait to hear all the details about your day when I get back. Bye now."

Her aunt's cheery voice was infectious.

At least Charlotte had her evening planned. Going to the show.

On her way to her bedroom, she stopped. The CD. In a flash, she dug it out of her purse and flew to the entertainment unit. The player wouldn't turn on fast enough. Sliding the CD in place, it receded into the stereo, and Charlotte cranked up the volume. The anticipation was high.

A bass shook the unit, followed by the guitar's entrance. The minor key colored each haunting note as it sang its sorrowful tune. Enhanced by the theatrical accompaniment, the music painted vivid, cinematic scenes in her mind.

She lay on the couch and read the booklet, surprised to see that Jesse had composed every track. The second song was a soft melody, but this time it featured his solo voice. She stared at the player, listening intently. She'd never heard him sing alone. He had a good voice. It wasn't powerful like Danny's, but it fit the music. Later, rock-like songs on the album with big drum fills showcased his voice as raw and gritty.

Charlotte squished her face in her hands, her cheeks sore from smiling. Pride swelled in her chest as the rest of his solo album played. The feeling was a bit absurd, given how little she knew him.

Wanting to arrive early for the interview, she freshened up, changed into a floral bodysuit, and pulled on black denim shorts with a black belt. She grabbed her purse and hailed a taxi to the Santa Monica Pier. This time, she wouldn't let her nerves get the better of her.

The musical entertainment was already in full swing by the time she arrived.

Wearing the lanyard Matt gave her, she slithered through the crowd and approached the side of the stage. "I'm here to meet with Matt Kendrick or Mr. Jackson," she told security.

Matt appeared from behind the canvas. "I'll take it from here."

Charlotte stepped beyond the roped-off section and let him guide her to the bearlike manager. J. J.'s smile was a relief as they shook hands.

"Good afternoon, Mr. Jackson," she said.

"Call me J. J."

"J. J., it is."

"The band is right back here." He led them to a small makeshift room behind a drape with chairs and benches.

They were all together. She grinned from ear to ear. Danny paced a little while, warming up his voice. Her heart fluttered.

Roy tapped his drumsticks against the back of a chair with over-the-top flair, hamming it up for Reggie, who watched with amusement. Scott and Mike sat in conversation with two women, quiet laughter between them. Off to the side, Jesse stood with a guitar slung over his shoulder, picking softly to himself, a grin on his lips as he took in Reggie and Roy's antics.

"Heads up guys, you didn't scare her off," J. J. joked, and they all turned in her direction. "And to grace us with his presence, Matty will be joining as a silent observer. You've got about twenty more minutes, then you need to get into position."

In the background, the crowd cheered for the group on stage.

The band greeted them warmly and introduced the women as Scott's and Mike's wives. They dressed for summer but were still elegant and chic, much like her aunt.

Matt hung back in a corner, quiet but unmistakable. His presence alone screamed for Charlotte to mess up again. She'd prove him wrong.

"I'm glad we didn't scare you off." Reggie offered her a seat between him and the drummer.

"We almost made a bet." Roy laughed out loud.

"It takes more to scare me away," Charlotte replied politely, tossing a look at Matt in the corner.

"Oh, she's got guts. I like that." Roy offered his fist, which she bumped.

"What do you got for us today, Charlotte?" Mike asked.

Charlotte cleared her throat and pulled out the CD and a marker. "First things first, I have to get the embarrassing request out of the way. Do you mind signing this CD for my friend Jason? He made this whole article happen."

Reggie, who sat next to her, snatched it playfully and started signing on the CD booklet. That was a relief.

"Anything for Jason," he said and passed the CD around.

"I appreciate it. Thank you." She pulled out her notebook with her questions. "We know the importance of music. What drew each of you to music? And what made it important for you? We'll start with Danny."

"When I was a kid, I loved listening to the choir at the church. The harmonies were fascinating. Then I started listening to blues which led into rock. It sucked me in, and the idea of blending blues, and rock sounds with intricate harmonies was fascinating to me," Danny spoke as he signed the album and then handed it to Scott, the rhythm guitarist.

His explanation made a whole lot of sense as several harmony sections from their music came to mind. Jesse took the album from Scott and signed it with his left hand. He was left-handed. She took note and jotted down the singer's answer with her own left hand. "Mike?"

He leaned back while rubbing his chin. "My mom dragged me to piano lessons, and I went kicking and screaming the first time. But when I started playing, it made sense. Like I said at our previous interview, it helped put things into perspective. Once it clicked, I poured myself into my lessons and consumed everything about theory and learning."

Scott pointed to himself. "I've always loved rock. Any and all rock groups: the Beatles, the Stones, Zeppelin, you name it. I wanted to be like them. I love everything about it."

With a smirk, Roy craned his neck over her shoulder as she scribbled everyone's answers. He waited until she was all caught up before he cleared his throat theatrically. "I couldn't sit still. I did everything from mowing lawns, cleaning out pools, hammering siding with my uncle and dad. Drove my mother crazy. It wasn't until my uncle took me to a rock show, then stuck some drumsticks in my hands, that I dived right in. Rock 'n' roll became my heartbeat. Being a drummer to get the chicks wasn't too bad either."

Charlotte turned to Jesse and locked eyes with him. "And you? What influenced you to play guitar?"

Jesse's expression softened. "My dad and grandfather were and still are musicians. I watched them and listened to everything they did. They loved a lot of different kinds of music, so I was exposed to all types. My grandfather owns a little recording studio, and I was always there grabbing every instrument I could get my hands on. The guitar won out."

Music ran in his family. Interesting. She could be musically inclined and didn't know it yet. She jotted down his answer.

Reggie spoke up, "Collectively we've made a conscious effort to stay away from the trends."

"That's true. Although it's healthy to always be fresh, following the next fad doesn't keep you relevant and can get you into trouble long term," Jesse said.

Reggie furthered, "We strive to make something unique that people want to hear and can connect with. That's always been our goal."

She finished writing their answers and smiled. "This sure is great. Now, I wanted to ask you about your thoughts on grunge music and how it's taken over the industry. Some bands have been madder than a hornet's nest calling it just another punk fad. And others have been really affected by it. What do you guys think of it?"

They all chuckled at her colorful description before Mike answered. "People hated rock 'n' roll when it first swept through the nation. You can't please everyone."

"Grunge has a real interesting sound. But it's not something we're going to follow," Scott said.

"Styles like the synthesizers or disco came and went, so to speak. Certain trends take a back seat, then come back. But we've found our fans like guitars and harmony. A live sound is appreciated rather than a carbon copy of what's on the album. The worst thing someone could say is that they could've stayed home and listened to the record," Danny stated.

"We like to give the crowd a great experience and stay true to our music and what we've created. Grunge is doing its thing, and that's great. We appreciate it. But Caravan's always been paving its own way, and that's what we'll keep doing," Mike finished with a smile.

Charlotte wrote down their answers in a flurry of sloppy pencil notes. "And should us fans expect any new music from Caravan?"

Jesse spoke up before anyone else. "We're planning to get into the studio in the next few weeks to play around with some new ideas."

From the corner of her eye, Charlotte caught movement. One of the women straightened, and the other folded her arms. Scott's nostrils flared, and Mike's eyes narrowed on Jesse. Reggie uncrossed and crossed his legs.

What happened? What changed?

Charlotte swallowed.

Jesse's fingers ran a quiet scale on the fretboard.

Matt shifted his weight in the corner.

Hurrying on to ease the mounting tension, she read the next question and laughed lightly. "Kind of a side question. My friend Jason wants to know about your hit single 'Fresh Poison.' Who wrote it?"

"I wrote the music," Jesse said at last. He pointed to the bass player and the singer. "These two wrote the words along with me."

"And what is 'Fresh Poison'?"

They traded glances and squirmed in their seats.

Reggie cleared his throat with a playful grin and leaned in. "You might say it's the aftereffects of tequila and vodka with um . . . acid."

Roy's brash voice spoke, "Waking up on the wrong side of a naked chick with a bad hangover."

"Roy!" He was admonished by one of the wives in the room.

Danny cleared his throat, and Mike swallowed as the wives adjusted in their seats.

Charlotte giggled. "I'll just put down 'open for interpretation.' " Everyone laughed. Roy snorted and high-fived Charlotte.

The interview came to a close, and the band agreed to take a photo with Charlotte. Matt stepped behind the canvas flap to avoid the picture, and one of the wives graciously took the photograph with a click of the camera.

As if on cue, their manager poked his round head into the makeshift room. "All right, guys. You're on in five."

Getting ready to take their place in the wing, they all said their thanks and goodbyes.

Reggie offered his fist again followed by Roy. "You're all right, Charlotte," Roy said.

She caught up with the singer before he left. "Hey, Danny, one last question. What's the one *thing* about making music to you?"

Danny's hands shook at his sides, most likely from mounting adrenaline. "Making music is about listening. Really listening. It's difficult sometimes with egos getting in the way." He chuckled. "Mine included. Listening to each other or taking on the perspective of the audience can be a long, tedious process, but it's essential for making good music the fans can resonate with. When you finally get it and you connect with the audience, it's the most powerful thing."

Matt opened the canvas flap signaling her to leave. Charlotte said firmly, "Thank you very much."

Danny squeezed her shoulder, said goodbye, and left.

Jesse removed the guitar from around his shoulder.

Before following Matt, Charlotte blurted out, "I bought your solo album today, *Moonlight*."

He laughed. "You're the one."

She humored him with a nervous grin. "It's so good. I didn't know you could sing so well. I mean, you sing very well on the album. I especially enjoyed 'Lovely' and 'Far from Home.' There were also some great guitar melodies."

His right dimple appeared with his smile. "Thanks, Charlotte." He paused. "Anyone ever call you Lotty?"

Charlotte's face dropped. "My best friend does."

"My grandmother's name was Charlotte. But the family always called her Lotty. Small world. See ya around." Waving goodbye, he slipped behind the curtain to join the rest of the band.

What did he just say? She stood blinking at the realization she could actually be named after Jesse's grandmother, her maybe great-grandmother.

One of the wives, a woman with a pixie face, short hair, and perfect skin, resembling Meg Ryan, stood and approached. "I sense someone is a little starstruck," she said.

Charlotte threw her hand up. "I'll admit it's hard not to make a fool of myself around Danny."

The woman laughed as she extended her hand. "Oh, no, you did great. I'm Jools, Mike's wife."

Charlotte took her hand. "It's nice to meet you officially."

"I'm Nicole," the other woman said. She had wavy, black hair, stylish glasses, and soft features. "I'm Scott's other half."

She was a dead ringer for the actress in that *Ghost* movie but with glasses, Charlotte thought. "Nice to meet you," she said. "Are there any more other halves?"

"Reggie's wife is taking care of a sick kid."

"Roy, Danny, and Jesse are the resident bachelors."

"Do you mind if I ask you ladies a few questions?" Charlotte ignored the sigh from behind her.

"Do we get to be in your article?" Jools raised an eyebrow with a playful grin.

"Sure," Charlotte said as she opened her notebook. "It's a question you get all the time, so we'll get it out of the way. What's it like being married to major rock stars like these guys?"

The muffled voice of the announcer introduced Caravan, and the crowd replied with deafening cheers. Jesse strummed the first note on his guitar. Roy kicked the bass drum, and it wasn't until Danny started singing that Jools turned to the teenager.

"It can have its moments. On stage, Mike is theirs, and they are Mike's. But when he is off stage, he is a husband and father. He mows the lawn, wears sweatpants, takes out the trash, and can be a slob sometimes." Jools chuckled.

"It can be difficult. Their absence is hard, but their return is cherished," Nicole said.

"I bet you like them touring locally," Charlotte stated as she wrote down their answers.

"Yes, it's been great," Nicole said.

"Seems like it's too good to be true," Jools spoke in a guarded tone.

Charlotte tilted her head to the side. "What do you mean?"

Jools stiffened and shifted her weight. "Oh, I wouldn't expect any new music anytime soon. That's all."

Charlotte frowned.

Nicole smiled. "Would you like to watch the show with us?"

"That'd be awesome. Thank you." Charlotte turned to the roadie. "Thanks, Matt. I won't be needing you any longer."

He shot her an icy look and muttered, "Whatever you say, your majesty," and disappeared behind the tent.

Filing out, the women guided her to the side of the stage. There was a clear view of the band.

Charlotte replayed Jools's statement. Tension in a band was normal. Bands had history. But Mike's wife had hinted at something deeper, something unsettled. What did she mean? And what did it mean for the band?

Chapter 9

Tension

Charlotte yawned and trudged into the pristine living room. The sun glistened on every glass surface. It was a palace. Out of habit, she turned on the television to listen to the MTV video countdown and poured a glass of orange juice.

After the show the night before, her aunt had been waiting for her and wanted all the juicy details. In turn, Charlotte asked her aunt to describe everything about her event and the beautiful models who walked the runway.

Although her aunt promised she was almost done with her commitments, Charlotte was a little bummed to be left alone again, especially on a weekend.

Leaning against the counter while the countdown played the "Mr. Jones" music video by Counting Crows, she picked up the phone. Her face lit as soon as she heard Jason's voice.

"Hiya Lotty, how's it going out there amongst the stars?"

"Like a dream. Getting to talk with the band was amazing. I got you a signed copy of one of their CDs. Roy wrote something inside. Don't let your mom see it."

Jason laughed. "That's awesome. Thanks."

"And guess what? Jesse is left-handed, just like me."

"Whoa, there's like approximately 10 percent of people who are left-handed."

"I know. And listen to this. He called me Lotty. That's his grandma's name."

"Did your mom name you after his grandmother?"

"It's getting freaky. But the good kind."

"So are you going to tell him at tonight's show?"

Charlotte slumped. "I want to get to know him a little bit more before I spring 'long-lost daughter' on him, but it's my last interview. It all happened so fast. What am I gonna do?"

"I don't know. If I think of something, I'll let you know."

"Thanks, Jase."

They chatted; he caught her up on small-town gossip while she shared about her Hollywood adventures. Jason promised to relay it back to their friends.

"What do you have going on today?"

"I'm going to call your cousin and annoy him a bit more."

"Aunt Heather told me she checked up with him. He said he's been an angel."

Her nose wrinkled, and she laughed. "An angel, huh? He might want to look up that definition in the dictionary. No, I'm kidding. He's been fun to mess with. It's all been so cool. I wish it wasn't Caravan's last night at the Pier and my final chance to ask questions. But I will see them again at the Hollywood Bowl. J. J. said he's giving me two tickets to their opening night. They've all been so nice."

"Any cool stories about them?"

"Reggie and Roy are wild and funny, a little like your friends Clint and Tanner. Mike, I sense, is kind of their leader holding them all together. I haven't quite pegged Scott yet."

"And your possible father?"

"He's quieter than I thought, a little more reserved. You wouldn't think that from seeing him on stage. He's a powerhouse out there. I gotta figure out how to get to know him more."

They both heard Jason's mom call for him to get off the phone because she was expecting a call. They said their goodbyes and hung up. The pad of her thumb rubbed the receiver, and she stared affectionately at the phone. It was good to hear his voice. What was he going to do for the rest of the day? Until now, they'd practically spent every moment together during their summer vacations. It was strange not seeing him on a regular basis.

Changing into a black cropped T-shirt with a design on the front and pairing it with some high-rise black denim shorts, she played Jesse's solo album again while making breakfast. Swaying to the beat, she let the music tug and pull at her emotions. Another swell of pride surged within her. He was so talented.

The phone rang.

She ran to the stereo, turned it off, then grabbed the receiver. "Becky Thompson's residence."

"Hey, you." Her mother's voice was on the other end.

"Hi, Mom." Charlotte smiled. "What's up?"

"I thought I'd call and see how the trip is going."

"It's going great. I'll be sending you some postcards today."

"Looking forward to them. Have you done any cool things with Aunt Becky?"

"Oh, yes. Aunt Becky took me all over Hollywood. It was incredible. And Los Angeles is so different from home. It's busy and fast paced. So many people." Charlotte regaled her with all the things she had seen and done.

"Wow, sounds like you've had a busy but fun time."

"I'm having a blast."

"Are you behaving and listening to Aunt Becky?"

"Tsk. I'm not a child but yes," Charlotte spoke playfully.

"More importantly, is Aunt Becky behaving herself?"

She giggled. "She's been good. Aunt Becky wants to take me to a fancy restaurant, and we're planning on seeing the Hollywood Sign and the observatory."

"You and that movie." Her mom chuckled.

Charlotte and Olivia loved the movie *Rebel Without a Cause* in which a portion of the movie was filmed at the Griffith Observatory. "I have to go there. Olivia would kill me if I didn't."

"I don't doubt it. I'm glad you're having a good time. It dawned on me the other day that this is the longest we've been away from each other. Ever."

Charlotte agreed.

A small pause hung between them before her mom concluded. "I just wanted to call and check in. Is Aunt Becky there?"

"No, she had a job thing."

"Give her my love. Tell her I'll call her later. I'll talk to you soon, okay?"

"All righty."

"Bye now."

Charlotte hung up. That was weird. Her mom had taken time out of her busy work schedule to call long-distance. But she didn't spend long dwelling on it as she walked to the post office to mail her postcards and the CD for Jason.

While talking with a postal worker about things to do in town, she advised the Beverly Center mall, an eight-story mall. Charlotte hailed a cab and paid the driver seven dollars when he dropped her off.

Going inside, she inhaled sharply. "Whoa." It was huge. They had a large mall back home, but the Beverly Center could house several of her town's malls. Music played over the speakers, a *shhhh* sound came from a fountain in the food court. Escalators crisscrossed above her, reaching for the sky, while a glass elevator glided silently between floors. Several levels housed countless shops like Whip Cream and Express, in addition to restaurants like the Hard Rock Cafe and Starsky's. In the center court, a huge wooden sculpture stood tall.

Shoppers weaved around each other, and Charlotte popped into Express. She goggled racks of denims and windbreakers.

On the fourth level, she leaned against the railing overlooking the food court. Several teens hung out together and held hands down there. She thought about her mom and aunt picking up boys. Super weird. What other kinds of things did her mom do when she was young? She'd have to find out. The idea of her mom catching rides with strangers was so foreign from the woman Charlotte knew now, but everyone kept saying the '70s was a different time.

Charlotte shook her head. The last interview already? Three interviews weren't enough. She needed more—needed to see Jesse again. But how? Jason had gotten her here, and she had to finish it. Somehow.

She wandered the mall a little more until her stomach grumbled, wishing she didn't have to eat alone. Finding a public phone, she dropped in a quarter to dial Matt's number, hoping he'd pick up. Saturday, it'd be a longshot.

To her surprise, he answered on the fifth ring. He'd had another late night but agreed to pick her up and take her for lunch. Bribing him with food seemed to work. The dwindling cash was worth it.

They went to the '50s diner again in West Hollywood for hamburgers. She didn't pass up the opportunity to pry him for more famous band details.

The conversation naturally steered toward Caravan. He worked behind the scenes. Did he ever witness any of the tension she had seen?

"I bet you've heard arguments from egotistical artists."

He nodded with his mouth full.

She leaned in. "Anyone in particular?"

He leaned forward on the table. "I'm not telling."

She pouted and slumped back in the booth. "You're no fun."

"It's not my place to listen nor do I care what they're yelling about. As long as they're not yelling at me, I keep my nose out of their business."

She tried again. "Can you nod your head if you've heard Caravan argue?"

He took an exaggerated gulp from his Coke, keeping her in avid suspense.

"Oh, come on. I won't tell anyone," she pleaded.

He stared out the window before lowering his voice. "All right. Yeah, I've heard them arguing. Some heated matches. One in particular was when I had to pick up some of Holt's specific amps he wanted for a benefit they were doing. They were all yelling."

"What about?"

"Don't know. Don't care. If I was with guys as many years as they've been together, I'd probably have a bone to pick with them too."

"It's times like this I find you absolutely useless." She pouted again.

Matt smirked. "You are something."

Her nose wrinkled at noticing the small foreign thing on his face. The hint of a smile. This was good.

The bill was paid, and Matt drove her to the Pier. The show didn't start for a while, so she used this time to walk barefoot on the beach. Her first West Coast beach experience. The hot sand tickled in between her toes, and the ankle-deep cold ocean water refreshed her feet.

She used up two rolls of film taking pictures of the surfers riding waves, people playing volleyball, and candid shots of people on the Pier. A father and his daughter stood in front of her in line for ice cream. After choosing a peaches and cream cone, she paid and meandered through the crowd, licking the sugary goodness. The energetic pace felt familiar now as she browsed the booths, buying a Caravan T-shirt as a memento.

Maybe she could catch J. J. and ask for a follow-up interview, like journalists did. Not a bad idea. She'd make a point to track him down before leaving the Pier.

The sunset became the musician's background, and the Pier grew packed with tourists and locals. Charlotte met Matt on the side, and she smiled brightly at his tight grimace before following him backstage. She'd almost had him at the restaurant. Now, he had reverted to being a grouch.

Walking backstage, she kept an eye out for J. J. He wasn't hard to spot in his Hawaiian button-down, standing by a stack of equipment cases in deep conversation with another man in a hat and glasses. Charlotte made a mental note of his location for later.

Matt stopped at the drape separating them from the band. J. J. was preoccupied, and Charlotte could see Matt didn't want to just enter.

Should they walk in? Should they announce themselves or wait for J. J.? There wasn't a place to knock. An idea came. She took out the T-shirt and stuck it through the slit in the drape. "We come in peace."

Matt rolled his eyes as laughter came from behind the drape. Jesse, with guitar slung in front of him, gestured her inside. "Hi, Charlotte. Matt." What was with him and his guitar? Was he permanently glued to the thing?

The interview breezed by. Too fast for Charlotte. By the time the band took their places in the wing, J. J. had vanished. Darn. Maybe if she lingered, he'd show up again. Much to Matt's chagrin, Charlotte turned to the wives with a huge grin and introduced herself to Reggie's wife, Madalen, a less glamorous, red-headed version of Julia Roberts. They made idle chitchat as the roar of the crowd commenced and the concert began.

Matt cleared his throat, reminding her of his reluctant presence.

"I'll be along in a minute, if you want to go." Charlotte gave him a cheery grin as he left. Breaking him was hard work.

"So do you have a favorite song of theirs, Charlotte?" Jools asked as she sipped from a water bottle.

"Oh, I don't know. I like a lot of them. A couple of the hits but mostly I like the lesser-known ones. 'Ploy,' 'Sugar Water,' and 'Poison and Roses' are good. Oh, and 'Tears from the Gallows' is mind-blowing. There's so many."

Madalen's red curls bobbed. "The older songs. I like that stuff too."

"Any song you absolutely can't stand?" Charlotte teased. "I promise not to tell."

Jools and Madalen exchanged glances before Jools answered. "There's a couple I'd be okay with never hearing again." She chuckled. "But that's my secret. Sorry."

Charlotte peeked out of the room and saw J. J. shaking hands with a few of the crew. Now was her chance. Quickly thanking the wives and saying goodbye, she rushed out of the little room. Stepping over a few cables and maneuvering around a stack of amp cases, she called out, "Mr. Jackson. I mean, J. J."

He turned toward her and clapped his meaty hands together. "Charlotte, I was coming to find you. How did your interviews go? Did you get enough for your article?"

"They went very well. Thank you so much for this opportunity. But about the article." A ball hitched in her throat.

From the breast pocket of his floral shirt, he pulled out two slips of paper. "Before I forget, I have two tickets for you. Opening night at the Hollywood Bowl."

Charlotte was in awe of the tickets in her hand. "This is incredible. Absolutely amazing. Thank you so much."

"They had some nice things to say about you."

"It's been so nice to get to know them too. But, Mr. Jackson, I mean, J. J. Do you think I could . . . I mean I don't want to impose, but could I get at least one more interview with them? Sort of like a follow-up one?"

J. J.'s grin grew big. "Funny you should ask. Look at your tickets."

Charlotte studied them further and saw that it said she had VIP backstage access.

"I think they like talking about themselves too much. They wanted to give you another opportunity to interview them."

Charlotte was speechless. Another chance. She had another chance. "Mr. J. J., I don't know what to say . . . words can't expre—Oh, thank you!"

His portly belly shook with laughter. "I expect Harrison High will keep their band program after your article. Well, the band shows up for sound check around three o'clock and takes about an hour. You can show up any time after that. If you have any questions, just call the box office. Nice meeting you, Charlotte."

Flying high, with Caravan's music ringing in her ears, she watched him disappear behind a drape. It felt as if life was laying all the pieces out just for her. The band wanted to see her again. Maybe he did too.

"He gave you the tickets."

Charlotte jumped from Matt's voice behind her. "Yes. He also gave me backstage passes. I get to hang out with them again. These precious little tickets are going in my notebook for safekeeping."

"You do that."

Rummaging through her bag, she couldn't find her notebook. "I think I left my notebook in their waiting area. I'll let you off the hook and go myself."

"When you come back, I'll make sure you get a taxi home."

"Why, Matt, do I hear concern in your voice?"

Matt waved a finger at her. "My mother called. Apparently, Jason keeps asking her to make sure I'm babysitting you."

"And you have to obey your mother. You're a good son." Charlotte snickered. "I'll meet you by the ropes."

Charlotte retraced her steps and approached the canvas drape. About to announce her presence, she paused. Voices filtered through the fabric. They were low and tense.

". . . Jesse thinks he can sweet-talk the band into dropping new music and going on tour. I've seen this before, and I won't let it happen."

It sounded like Jools. Charlotte bit her lip, unable to resist overhearing. What did she say about Jesse? Glancing over her shoulder to make sure the coast was clear, she edged closer to the drape.

"I love him," another voice replied. "But he and Scott can be pompous jerks."

"Scott wants to go on tour too?" Jools's voice sounded irritated.

"Well, he wants to be the one in charge and make the decisions. Jesse is better at it than him. So they lock horns. I'm sick and tired of hearing the same old fights."

Charlotte's chest tightened. She hadn't expected to hear this. This was awkward. How could she get her notebook now?

Madalen's voice chimed in, "They've paid their dues and should take a break. Jesse doesn't see it that way. He's way too driven."

"Oh, look. I think that's Charlotte's notebook. I'll see if I can catch her."

With quick thinking on her part, Charlotte ran back several feet, then sauntered up toward the drape as Jools slipped through, making it appear as if she had just arrived.

Charlotte plastered a fake smile on her face. "There it is. Jason would've killed me if I lost it."

"I was just coming to find you." Jools handed it to her.

With a quick glance, Charlotte saw all three women with pleasant expressions, like they hadn't even had such a tense conversation. It was freaky. She thanked them for her notebook and went back to the ropes.

While waiting for Matt, she watched the show but couldn't enjoy it. Everything the women had said swirled in her head. Her eyes never left Jesse. Driven? Jesse and Scott locked in conflict? They hid it well up there on stage.

She couldn't understand it. They were a rock band. They're supposed to make music. Why were the wives so upset? The tension behind the music was real and more complicated than she imagined.

When Charlotte arrived back at the apartment, Aunt Becky was on the phone laughing with her cheery laugh.

"Oh, there she is," Becky said with a sparkling smile on her face. "Charlotte's just walked in."

Charlotte hung up her purse and kicked off her shoes. "Who is it?"

"It's your mother. . . . Yes, she's right here. Oh, stop worrying. It's not that late, and she's home safe and sound. I bet she had the time of her life." She laughed again and handed the phone to Charlotte. "Want to talk to your mom?"

Charlotte looked at her watch. It must be late back home. "Hi, Mom."

"Hi, hon. Did you have fun tonight?"

"Yep. I went to the Pier with Matt. Mrs. Kendrick told you he'd be looking out for me out here." This answer seemed to relieve her mom's suspicions a little.

"I'm just concerned you being out so late."

"Mom, it's nine thirty. There's no need to go mental on me."

"I just want you safe."

"I'm not wandering the streets at night by myself. Matt was at the show and made sure I got to the taxi safe and sound."

"Well, I'm glad you had a good time tonight."

"Thank you."

"Call me in a couple days."

"Will do."

"It's quite late here. I'll let you guys go. Say goodbye to Becky for me."

"All right. Bye." Charlotte hung up the phone. "Mom says bye."

"Got a little chilly there," Aunt Becky said, then sipped on her wine.

Charlotte rolled her eyes. "Mom can get a little paranoid, but not once have I ever done anything to make her think she can't trust me."

"She just loves you."

"I know."

"Well, she and I had a nice chat." Aunt Becky floated over to the couch. "Now, little miss thing, I want to hear everything you did today. Don't leave anything out."

"I've been exploring LA, going to the Beverly Center. Your mall is so huge. Matt met me for lunch. We went to the beach and listened to some live music on the Pier. It was a blast. The crowd was amazing. So full of life."

"Welcome to California."

"What about you, Aunt Becky? What happened with you today? Are we painting the town tomorrow?"

"Oh, the shoot was incredible. But my boss wants me to oversee some of the developments."

"On a Sunday?"

"I think he wants me there to yell at me if any of the photographs turn out bad."

"Sounds harsh."

"Then Monday morning, I'll have a quick stay at the office, but after that, I'm all yours. I've reservations Monday night for Chasen's, the fancy restaurant."

In her big, pillowy bed, Charlotte's body ached from the long day, but her mind refused to rest. Jools's words replayed over in her mind, angry and irritated. Charlotte understood the wives had a history with the band. But still, hearing Jesse described as the problem pulled at her chest in a way she hadn't expected.

Why did it bother her?

If he was so driven, why did he push the band so relentlessly?

She didn't want to believe he was the source of the tension, yet she couldn't ignore the possibility. Rock stars weren't squeaky clean just because they made good music.

An uncomfortable thought crept into her mind. Should she be angry that he'd built this amazing life of fame and fortune while she and her mom went it alone? She didn't know how to feel, and the uncertainty made her wince.

Charlotte rolled onto her side and hugged a second pillow to her chest. She barely knew him. She had to keep reminding herself of that. Yet the questions kept coming about the band, about Jesse, and about what it meant to want something badly enough to risk losing everything else.

Chapter 10

The Apple Pan

Charlotte waited at the bus stop a short distance from the apartment. Matt was busy with his job, and Aunt Becky had to finish up her last-minute things. Tired of being cooped up in the apartment, she wanted to experience something new. The city bus. And she knew exactly where to go. For pie.

Matt had mentioned a few different pie places, and Charlotte decided on The Apple Pan. She looked up its address and deciphered the bus route she would need to take. It was thrilling to wait on the bench down the street from the apartment. She chewed on some bubble gum as the cars flew by. Finally, the bus arrived on time, and she hopped up as the brakes screeched to a halt.

Taking a window seat right behind the bus driver, she glued her face to the glass as the city went by. She prided herself on her directions to the second and third bus stops. Being let out at Pico Boulevard and Westwood Boulevard, she confirmed with the driver that the restaurant was only a minute away. She arrived in front of the cutest little building with a white exterior and a green roof and trim. The sign out front read "The Apple Pan Quality Forever." It reminded Charlotte of home, an almost Southern style place serving comfort food. She snapped a picture.

The inside was small. Barstools lined a curved bar top that faced the kitchen. That was it. The only seating in the whole place. A handful of customers took up a few of the barstools. Charlotte noticed a sign on the wall explaining the seating rules of the tiny diner. The last rule made her grin. "Don't leave an empty space when you take your seat. You never know who you're going to meet!"

Following the rules, Charlotte took up a seat against the wall. The cooks worked tirelessly behind the red brick grill. The waitress brought her a tea, and Charlotte read the menu.

The door swung open, and she shot a look in that direction. She did a double take. "No way," she said under her breath as none other than Jesse Holt walked inside.

He removed his sunglasses and hung them on his shirt as he greeted the waitstaff.

Charlotte didn't know what to do. Did she wave and greet him? Would he be bothered by her? Her questions halted when he caught her eyes, his expression lit up as he approached her. "Miss Reynolds, fancy meeting you here."

She nodded. The butterflies in her stomach fluttered. Never in her wildest dreams did she think that the sign would come to fruition. "Hi," she croaked out.

"May I join you?"

"Sure."

How was this possible? Jesse Holt was sitting next to her.

"What brings you to The Apple Pan?" he said as he asked for coffee.

"I heard this was a good place for pie. I've never been."

"Oh, you came to the best place. This is the only spot to go for pie."

"Have you come here a lot?"

"Every year." He took a cautious sip of the steaming coffee.

Charlotte glanced at the menu. "Since you're the expert, what's the best pie here?"

He grinned like a little kid as he pointed to the flavor.

Her jaw dropped. "Boysenberry."

"It's my favorite."

"Mine too," Charlotte stammered.

The waitress came, and they both ordered the same flavor.

"So, Miss Reynolds, did you get enough information for your article?"

Charlotte took a drink from her tea. "Almost. Mr. Jackson informed me you all gave me backstage passes for your next concert. I can't thank you enough."

"This is a big deal for us. We're pretty passionate about music in school. So we'll be ready for more of you and your insightful questions." He took another sip from his cup. "Be honest. This paper you're doing. Out of all your classmates, you drew the short straw, didn't you."

A twinge of guilt rose up in her chest, but she stuffed it back down. "I liked the idea. My uh . . . teacher is a fan. And she thought it'd be good to interview you all for the arts and stuff. And I'm a major fan now."

"Uh-huh. Sure," he teased.

Accepting the challenge, Charlotte shifted in her seat. "I really like 'Ploy' off your debut album and 'Dangerous Game' from the B side of your third album, *Passages*."

"You know your stuff."

"What struck me about your band is the skill level from your first album. You were all so young but talented. Like real musicians. I listened to your fifth album, *Here We Go*, first, then went back to the first one expecting it to be eh—just all right. But I was surprised as all get out that the skill level was still on par. Each album was fresh and new and exciting."

Jesse nodded. "Why, thank you."

"Your guitar playing is mind-blowing. You create these melodies that are hummable. I find myself humming them, and not just Danny's parts. They get stuck in my head, in the good kind of way. Whatever you do is genius."

His right dimple appeared as he grinned. "Miss Reynolds, you are a well-informed journalist."

"So would you say I'm a legit fan?"

He dubbed her with his fork. "Welcome to the fandom."

The server brought out two huge slices of boysenberry pie, and they ate a few bites in silence.

"Oh, wow," Charlotte said. It was so gooey and warm. Tangy and sweet on her tongue.

"My grandmother and I would get several different flavors and share. But I'd usually just eat the boysenberry."

"Is she the grandma named Charlotte?"

He nodded and chewed on the flaky crust.

"Your grandmother will be upset with you for sneaking a slice without her."

"She passed away a few years back."

Charlotte stopped chewing. Oops. "Sorry."

"I still come here if I can. It was a tradition."

"That's nice." Charlotte took another bite, then gasped, "Wait a minute. Tradition. Is today your birthday?! Oh, my gosh. It is, isn't it?" Several of the entertainment issues from the library back home listed his birthday as June 27. Today. "You come here on your birthday."

He pointed his fork at her. "You would make a good detective."

Birthdays meant something to her. Sitting now with her possible father, she wondered what it would've been like to have him there each year to watch her blow out the candles. He ate pie every year for his birthday with his family. She spent her birthdays longing and dreaming.

Charlotte swallowed. "So, it's your birthday. Which one is it?"

He hesitated.

"Are you one of those who doesn't like giving out their age?" she teased.

He finally admitted the number, "I'm thirty-nine."

"That's not so bad."

He and her mom were a couple of years apart.

Staring mindlessly at the brick grill, he said, "It's hard to imagine we started almost twenty years ago. Time goes by faster as you get older."

"You're one depressing dude." She smirked.

"Sorry."

A mom with her teenage daughter approached them with a hushed tone. "Excuse me, you're Jesse Holt, aren't you?"

He hesitated to answer before inevitably confirming the fan's suspicions and shaking her hand.

"Oh, my gosh, I have been a huge fan all these years. I've gone to so many of your shows. I lost count."

He gave a warm greeting. "Thank you. That means a lot."

"I can't believe I ran into you here."

Jesse politely gestured to the mother's daughter. "Is this your daughter?"

"Yes, her name is Jill."

Jesse nodded at the daughter who made it obvious she didn't care who he was or anything about him. The mom rummaged through her purse. "I don't have a piece of paper. Could you sign something for me? If I can find something. Where's that receipt?"

Charlotte handed the bumbling woman a clean napkin. "Will this do?"

"Thanks." The woman took it and, with a trembling hand, gave it to the musician. "Could you sign this for me?"

"Of course." He waited patiently as she fumbled for a pen in her purse. "And what's your name?"

"Oh, my gosh. Cheryl. Cheryl Myers. I have all of your albums. I've probably worn them out."

"I appreciate it. What are you and your daughter doing today?"

"Um, we're uh . . . we're out shopping. Having a mother-daughter day."

Charlotte exchanged glances with Jill, the daughter, who rolled her eyes and hitched a hand on her hip. It had been years since Charlotte had a mother-daughter day with her own mom. Why couldn't she take just a day off and spend time with her? This Jill didn't know what she had was special.

Jesse handed the napkin back. "You and your daughter have a nice day."

"Thank you. Thank you so much. It was so nice to meet you." Cheryl shook his hand.

"Come on, Mom. Let's go." Jill's voice was laced with annoyance. Cheryl walked out with her daughter listening to her go on about the musician.

A few of the other customers' stares lingered on them. Charlotte giggled. "Now I have to ask. Craziest fan experience?"

He put his fork in his mouth while thinking, then spoke. "A few girls pretended to be maids at the hotel we were staying at so they could get into our room. That's probably one of the most creative."

"No way."

"Uniforms, a cart, the works."

Charlotte gasped, "Did it work?"

"No. Our security noticed they looked a little too young."

Charlotte shook her head in amazement. "I've never been like that about anybody."

"Those were some crazy times."

Charlotte sipped her tea and chewed her ice, then asked, "I have another question."

"Is this on the record?" He gave a silly grin.

"This is purely for selfish reasons. My question. And it's an extremely important one. Did you beat up a kid who was bullying another?"

Jesse scrunched his face and shook his head. "What?"

Charlotte couldn't help laughing. "I read an OLD *Teen Beat* magazine on you guys, and it said you are loyal to a fault and protect your friends and mentioned the beating up of the bully from some school."

Jesse laughed. "Well, thanks for emphasizing the article was old, but I never beat up a bully."

Charlotte made a face. "That's kind of a bummer. Guess you're not as cool as the article claimed," she joked.

"Hey now. I did rough up some kid messing with my brother when we were kids. But that's all."

"I guess that's kind of cool."

"Sorry I disappointed you. But that stuff is all bull—" He stopped. "Crap."

Charlotte snorted. "So how long had you been playing before you joined the band?"

Jesse scrunched his face. "Whew. Well, my mom gave me my first record when I was nine or ten. It was the Yardbirds album *For Your Love*, and I was hooked. Speaking of birthdays, my dad gave me my first guitar and taught me a few chords. Then my grandfather helped me a little with music theory. But the rest was years of dissecting great music and learning from the best."

He was close with his family.

"And so, you guys formed the group, and a star was born."

"Not exactly. We worked hard, traveled a lot. Stayed in dingy hotels. Played in front of any crowd we could just to play and get our name out there."

"But you guys were stars."

"Nope."

"I mean, your debut album was super successful."

"Not quite. It took a lot of years and several albums and tours before we got the kind of success I think you are equating us with. We opened for several headliners for a few years before we were able to headline ourselves."

Those articles reported about them being successful and famous with gold and multi-platinum albums. She never imagined the time it took to get there. "Hmm." Her tea was refilled by the waitress. "Do you have any suggestions on good '70s and '80s music? I trust you, being a professional musician and all." She savored every little piece of her pie.

Jesse blinked up at the ceiling. "Um, you might try Free, Little River Band, or Southside Johnny and The Asbury Jukes. If you want old rock, listen to Jimi Hendrix or The Who and Thin Lizzy. And of course, The Yardbirds and The Allman Brothers are pretty great."

Some of the bands he mentioned sounded familiar, and she was excited to be educated in good music.

"What kind of music are you kids listening to nowadays?"

Charlotte clasped her hands to her chest with excitement. "Everything Nirvana. They are totally amazing. Counting Crows is not too bad. Oh, and Pearl Jam's album *Vs.* is so good."

Jesse made a face. "Grunge music, huh."

Charlotte shrugged. "It's not bad. It's what's new right now."

"My niece enjoys that kind of music. She's a few years younger than you. You remind me a little of her actually."

Charlotte's cheeks grew hot. "I like your era too—Aerosmith and Led Zeppelin. I was surprised. I've actually heard a few of you guys' songs on the radio. I never knew it was you. Do you ever change the channel when you hear yourself on the radio?"

Jesse chuckled. "Can't hit the button fast enough. It'd be weird if I didn't, don't you think? I mean, I like the songs we play, and I appreciate the airplay, but it seems a bit narcissistic."

"Let's be honest, I think you have to be a little bit of one to be in the business you're in," Charlotte teased.

His jaw dropped in mock offense.

"What do you listen to? As a famous rock musician, I'm slightly curious."

"I love all kinds of music. Classical, jazz, blues especially, rock. Even some opera. You name it."

Charlotte rolled her eyes. "Opera. Ick."

"Don't knock it till you've heard it."

"I've heard all I want to hear. My friend Olivia loves it. I don't understand her sometimes." She giggled. "Didn't peg you as someone who liked that kind of stuff too."

"All different kinds of music, including opera, can make you feel something. Depends on what mood you're in or want to be in."

She sensed a double meaning in what he said. "And what mood are you in today?"

He turned and smiled. "Having a blast."

She didn't quite believe him but couldn't put her finger on it. "Are you guys excited about playing the Hollywood Bowl?"

"Yep, any chance to play for a crowd is great."

"Do you always play the same show?"

"No, we're going into the rehearsal studio tomorrow to switch things up a bit. The Bowl is where we're doing a full set. We're going to play around with a few new songs."

"That's so cool."

"If you want to sit in, you're welcome too. Get in a few more questions. I'm expecting a highly detailed article."

Her eyebrows rose. Was he asking to spend more time with her? She responded tactfully. "Well, I wouldn't want to intrude or annoy you guys with my presence."

"We like you."

Charlotte's heart swelled. "All righty then. Thanks. I'll come." There was some small part of her that felt bad for lying about the article. But the excuse allowed her to see him again.

They talked a little more when the waitress dropped off their bill. She insisted on paying for herself, but he paid for it.

He opened the green door for her and put on his sunglasses. She almost didn't want this to end. Every minute with him gave her more insight into who he was.

"Is your mom picking you up?"

"No. I'm going to take the bus."

He stopped, and his eyebrows rose over his sunglasses. "The bus?"

"I'm new to the area and trying new things. It was fun."

He chuckled at her enthusiasm, then looked at his watch. "Look, I have a radio interview to get to, but would you like me to drop you off on my way?"

Charlotte shook her head. "I couldn't impose."

"It's not imposing."

"Well, it'll save me a couple bucks on bus fare."

He led her around the block to a dark green convertible.

Charlotte marveled at the slick paint job and the Corvette emblem. "Is this your car?!"

He opened the door for her. "Yep. I got it back in 1980 when it was brand new. It's my pride and joy."

"You're one of those rock 'n' roll guys who's obsessed with cars, aren't you?" She slid into the bucket seat.

"You might say that." His smile was big as he shut her door and slid into the driver's side.

"This is a really cool car. Jason is going to have a cow when he finds out."

Jesse brought the engine to life, put the car in gear, and turned onto Pico Boulevard, then Veteran Avenue.

Her hair blew in the wind, and she didn't care. This was the happiest moment of her life.

"You said you're new here. Where did you move from?"

"Oak Falls, South Carolina."

"What's it like there?"

"Slower paced. There's mountains and trees but not like here. It's a different energy there. Like something out of a storybook, I guess."

"Why did you move out here?"

Charlotte ran through several excuses in her head within a split second. "The same old story. Better opportunities."

"It must be tough being away from all your family."

"I don't have a ton of family. Just my mom and me. But I also have my best friend, Jason."

They came to a stop, and she stared at the red light as an ache rose in her chest. Being away from Jason was hard; he'd become almost a permanent fixture in her life. Leaving him just to travel all the time felt unthinkable. How did musicians tour for months at a time, away from the people they loved? How did *he* do it?

"Why do you do it? Travel so much, make music. What's the reason?"

"Seeing all those faces of people being happy. Forgetting all their troubles. Feeling no pain. In tune right there with me on that same high. Connecting. It's the best feeling in the world. It's incredible. There's no other feeling like it."

Was it better than having a family? Having a daughter?

He pulled up to the curb in front of her apartment building. She didn't want to leave. For a split second, the truth pressed hard against her lips—I am your daughter. But somehow telling him here on the street felt wrong. Or maybe that was just an excuse. Maybe she was chickening out.

Being with him was the best feeling she'd had in a long time, but her aunt would be home by now, and she couldn't keep her waiting. So she shut the car door, telling herself she'd see him at the rehearsal the next day.

"Do you have any exciting birthday plans, or are you going to be a boring adult about it?"

He adjusted his sunglasses. "I'm stopping by my parents tonight, as per my mother's request."

"Oh, good. It's good to spend birthdays with your family. Well, thanks for the ride. I appreciate it."

"See you around, Charlotte. You made this day special."

With that, he drove off.

When entering the apartment, Aunt Becky whirled around from the kitchen island. "Hey, girl."

"You're back," Charlotte exclaimed excitedly.

"I got home a few minutes ago."

"Perfect timing."

"Did you have fun with your friend?"

"Yes. My friend. Yep. We had fun." She was getting good at little white lies.

"Did you get him to smile yet?"

"There was the tiniest smile from him. I think I'm getting to him." She flopped on the couch, and her aunt joined her.

"Did you eat some lunch?"

"Actually. All I had was pie."

"That's not lunch. We'll make you a sandwich, then I'm whisking you away. Tonight is dinner with the stars. Well, hopefully, we'll see one or two celebrities while we eat. But first, I need to buy you an appropriate dress. Let's go shopping."

❖ ❖ ❖

That evening, Charlotte and Aunt Becky arrived at Chasen's restaurant in West Hollywood and were ushered to a circular booth, dripping with a creamy tablecloth. In a floor-length black satin evening dress with straps wrapped around her neck, Charlotte felt like royalty. Aunt Becky wore a deep red dress that hugged her hourglass frame. They clutched their handbags and situated themselves into the booth.

The cloth napkins were as smooth as butter, and the silverware must have been real silver. The moody ambience permeated the air with a sense of exclusivity. Its rich wood paneling, plush seating, and warm light created an inviting atmosphere.

"You've got to have their signature chili. It was Elizabeth Taylor's favorite."

"Deal." Charlotte took a sip of chilled water from her fluted glass after a waiter in a tailored suit poured it for her. Aunt Becky ordered the salmon and Charlotte the chili.

Charlotte discreetly glanced around, then leaned forward and whispered, "Aunt Becky! That's Robert DeNiro."

Aunt Becky grinned and spoke low, "And Meryl Streep is two tables behind you."

Charlotte bit her lip to keep from screaming. She pretended to drop her napkin from her lap. When retrieving it, she spied the famous actress. "This is incredible. This has been the best summer of my entire life."

"What do your summers usually look like?"

"Spending them mostly with Jason and working at the video store. Sometimes Jason and his family take me with them to Myrtle Beach."

"Lori doesn't go with?"

Charlotte shook her head. "She hasn't gone to the beach since I was six."

"That's surprising. We loved the beach out here."

"Yeah, well, my mom isn't quite the same person she was growing up. I'm finding that out."

"She works real hard."

"Oh, I know. So that we can keep the roof over our heads."

"I hear she is quite successful, not just in Oak Falls."

"She's sold several houses in the surrounding cities." Charlotte didn't mention how it meant she traveled a lot, leaving little time for her own daughter.

Aunt Becky drank her chilled tea. "It's amazing to see how far your mom has come. There were many teary, long-distance calls while she worked to get her license. You were just a baby." She grinned from ear to ear. "You were so pink and chunky. When I visited, I held you in my arms, never imagining the beautiful woman you'd grow into. You're the best a godmother could ask for."

Their food arrived, and the rest of the evening was full of eye-spying Hollywood stars and confirming upcoming events. As they finished memorable meals, Aunt Becky said, "After my hair appointment tomorrow, we'll party like it's 1969!"

Chapter 11

Recording Studio

"Jason, it has been the most exciting last few days. I can't begin to describe it." Charlotte paced the living room while holding the wireless receiver against her ear. The details about her experiences were laid out along with the one-on-one time with her dad.

"I can't believe you got to ride in his Corvette."

"That's what you took from the conversation?"

"Well, yeah."

"Did you get the package? I sent it priority."

"Yes. Thanks for the signed CD. Roy's note is hilarious."

"He's pretty funny. Oh, Jason. It's been the absolute best. I can't believe it. It feels like a dream. Jesse is the coolest and nicest guy." She paused before rushing on. "But I don't know. I got this feeling that he's a bit sad. I mean, it was his birthday, and he went to the pie shop alone to honor his grandmother."

"You said he was going to spend time with his family that night. He's fine."

She tapped her finger on the phone. "All this makes me wonder about things. How do I even talk to someone like him about me, his daughter? And when do I spring it on him? What if he doesn't even want to know me at all? He's busy being famous and, well, what if he'd eventually distance himself from me, just like my mom does. If he even wants me at all."

"I'm sure he just doesn't know you exist. He'd be crazy not to want to have you as his daughter. You're pretty great."

She sank into the couch. "Thanks, Jase." The rest of their few precious minutes were spent talking about Chasen's and the glamorous celebrities they saw.

"After this, you're not gonna want to come home."

"That's not true."

"Charlotte Reynolds, the glamorous daughter of a rock star living the highlife. Forgetting all about the little people back home."

"Jason Hunter, you stop that." She giggled. "I'd never forget you."

There was a pause on the phone before he spoke. "I do miss you. Summer's been kind of boring without you."

"Well, good. A little missing isn't a bad thing."

"Do you miss me?"

"Of course, I miss you. What a silly question." Charlotte's expression softened.

The silence lingered between them. It felt easy. The kind they used to share walking downtown back home while passing the white dogwood trees nestled between red brick buildings. Jason always insisted on walking closest to the street, claiming it was the gentlemanly thing to do. The memory of those quiet walks made her smile.

Jason cleared his throat. "Great . . . uh. So when does your aunt get back from the hairdresser?"

"Closer to noon."

"You didn't want to go?"

"I don't mind getting my nails done but sit for hours for a blowout and style? No, thanks. I told her Matt was taking me to get some ice cream, then I'd be back. What she doesn't know is that Jesse invited me to sit in on their rehearsal this morning."

"No way! You get to sit in on a rehearsal? That's always been something on my wish list, and here you are getting to do it."

"I don't think they're recording anything, just practicing for their concert. But I am meeting them at a studio."

"Like the one Olivia's sung at?"

"I reckon so."

"I want to know everything. What the studio looks like, smells like, down to the last detail. And maybe ask them what other famous musicians have recorded there. What's the name of it? Is it one of the famous ones?"

"Slow down now. Who'd of thought Jason Hunter would geek out over such a thing as a recording studio."

"Recording studios have history. If only those walls could talk."

"I promise I'll tell you every little thing. And maybe take pictures if they'll let me."

"Oh, and since you have a few more chances with them, I got some more questions for you I stole from other journalists or past interviewers that don't suck. Got a pen?"

"Yep."

Jason rattled off a list as Charlotte wrote them down in her notebook. "These are great, Jason. Thanks."

"No problem."

"How's working at Hollywood Video?"

"Eh. Boring sometimes. Our friends pop in a lot, and the money is nice. Oh, I finally did a Casper flip on the skateboard."

"No way," Charlotte exclaimed. He had spent many hours at the skate park attempting the technical move. "Jason, that's awesome." Her lips pursed. "I'm sorry I missed it."

"It'll give me time to master it before you get back."

"Deal." She listened to him catch her up on all the latest gossip. Two of their friends who were dating broke up with each other. Another friend broke an arm at the skate park, and old Mr. Gentry from the senior center passed away.

"Oh, that's too bad." She used to send him hand-painted birthday cards.

"He had a good turnout at his funeral. My family went. Your mom was there."

"Oh, good. He was a nice man."

"He still had several of the cards hung up in his room."

A tear slid down her cheek. "That's so sweet."

The clock read nine thirty.

"I've got to go if I want to make it to their rehearsal, and I can't raise Aunt Becky's phone bill."

"Tell me everything."

Charlotte laughed. "It'll be like you're there. Bye."

She hung up the phone, wishing he was going with her to the studio. It was weird not experiencing their summer days together. Changing into a pair of denim shorts and an '80s band T-shirt, she ordered a cab to the studio.

It was . . . a bit disappointing.

A plain brown brick building. It was disguised as a normal business among all the other surrounding businesses, a one-level structure with double glass doors and a sign out front, "Sound Sessions Studio."

She half-expected it to look like the Sun Studio in Memphis with its iconic record logo on the side of the building. This building was plain old boring.

Reluctantly, after taking a picture of the ordinary sign for Jason, she went inside. Soft blue walls, fluorescent lights, and a few large potted plants on the floor were the foyer's decor. Just as boring as the outside.

A secretary looked up from behind the curved front desk. "How can I help you today?" she greeted warmly.

Beyond the desk was a set of double doors. Charlotte gave the woman her name and was relieved to be on the approval list. The secretary gestured for Charlotte to enter the double doors.

The building went deeper than she originally imagined. Rows of doors lined either side of the brown paneled hallway. Years of stale cigarette smoke hung in the air, and she scrunched her nose. Dim fluorescent lighting further revealed the orange tint from the ashy vapor stains on the paneling. This place hadn't been updated since the '70s, maybe even the '60s. Yet there was a certain charm about it. It was like a time capsule. Frozen in years gone by.

Charlotte kept checking for the correct door and paused when muffled voices came from down the hall, the voices of Mike and

Danny. The door stood ajar and, when she was about to open it, a heated exchange inside made her stop.

". . . Princess decided to grace us with her presence," Scott clipped.

"Did someone not have their coffee yet?" Jesse lathered on the sarcasm.

"Rehearsals were for nine, man." Danny's voice was calm but held some irritation.

"Sorry, I had a late night."

"Oh, yeah," Roy bellowed with cheer. "The big four-o with the family."

"Thirty-nine, but yes."

Scott's dark voice spoke, "It seems you were full of surprises yesterday."

"Are we going to speak in half riddles all day?"

Mike exhaled as he adjusted his glasses. "We heard it, Jesse. We heard you on the radio."

"And J. J. isn't happy with you," Scott interjected. "He tried to reach you."

"You can't be making bold claims like that without our consent or J. J.'s approval," Mike stated.

"I'll smooth things over with him," Jesse said.

"Sure you will, 'cause you always have him wrapped around your finger," Scott scoffed.

"Do you need to get something off your chest, Scotty?" Jesse asked.

"What possessed you to say we were working on a new album?" Scott shook his head.

"Let alone plans for another tour," Danny spoke up.

Reggie chimed in, "For the record, I'm not as heated as them. I'd actually prefer to keep busy."

Jesse rubbed his forehead and tightened his lips. "They asked if we were working on new material. What am I gonna say, no? We always are."

"You have excuses for everything," Scott said.

"I don't understand the problem. J. J. arranged this interview. I said what we've always said in interviews. You're acting like I kicked your dog."

"To talk about the Hollywood Bowl! Not a massive, long tour promoting a new album," Scott yelled.

Charlotte almost jumped at the anger in his voice.

"We agreed to cool it for a while after this run," Mike said calmly.

Danny cleared his throat. "I'm tired. My voice is about shot."

"And while on break, we can write some new material. Nothing new here," Jesse stated.

Mike spoke emphatically, "Jesse, we're going to run ourselves into the ground if we don't take a break."

"I get it, but we've got to remember if we don't stay on our game, twenty more bands will take our place. Our last album didn't do so hot. This new wave of music is killing us."

"You have a pretty low view of our fans," Scott said.

"I've never said that," Jesse replied.

Reggie pointed to himself. "I'm always down for another tour. Whatever gets me out of the house."

Roy shrugged. "I'll do whatever."

Scott raised his voice. "We're selling out the Hollywood Bowl and adding more shows to accommodate, and we have a big interview lined up with Leno. Seems to me we're still on top. This is you trying to manipulate us to do your bidding."

"Excuse me?" Jesse's tone warned the rhythm guitarist.

"Oh, boy." Reggie face-palmed.

"Mom and Dad are fighting again." Roy turned to the bass player.

"Okay, let's just cool it." Mike refereed the argument.

"Who am I trying to manipulate, Scotty? Huh? Who? And to do what exactly?"

"You seem to forget that Mike and I asked you to join our band, you've—"

"Your band?" Danny asked.

"Yes, our band," Scott continued. "The past few years you've been trying to control every aspect of it. You got our manager to side with you, not to mention Roy and Reggie, who you manipulate for your purposes."

Roy straightened. "I resent you saying I'm easily manipulated."

Reggie leaned toward the drummer. "Do you deny it?"

"No, I just resent it," Roy said. He and Reggie both chuckled.

Jesse's eyes narrowed. "I seem to remember you begging me to join *your* band."

Reggie raised his hand. "I'd like to get off this merry-go-round, and I would like a refund."

"Guys, enough," Mike warned.

"If this is your band, Scott, then by all means take it." Danny's voice was testy.

"Mike and I started this band." Scott jabbed a finger toward the guitarist. "And you are ripping it apart because you can't get your head out of your own ego."

"Scott, shut up," Mike said.

"I was wrong. You've had enough coffee," Jesse said.

"You're so infuriating," Scott seethed.

"And I like my head where it's at, thank you very much," Jesse said.

"Whew, and I thought the fights Madalen and I have gotten into were bad," Reggie half joked.

For the first time everyone shut up and turned to face him.

With all eyes on him, the bass player elaborated. "We read the writing on the wall. We're going our separate ways. So there's that." His voice sounded a little sad.

Silence.

Charlotte covered her mouth. There was no way she would go into that room now.

"Excuse me, can I help you?"

Charlotte jumped and turned to a man with a receding hairline and big fat glasses. He wore faded jeans and a T-shirt and held a coffee mug. "Hi . . . the band . . . Caravan. Jesse, Mike, and the others were expecting me. If you want to check, I'm on the list out front."

With a grin, he took a sip from his cup. "Well, if you're on the list, then you're on the list." He opened the door, oblivious to what had transpired inside. "Hey, guys. I found this young lady outside. She's on the list."

Charlotte reluctantly followed behind him and meekly waved. The man with the coffee cup must have been their sound engineer because he went behind a sound board.

Thick tension hung in the air. Each band member had a good distance between them. Behind his drum kit, Roy gave Charlotte a big smile and waved with the stick in hand. He didn't seem to be affected by the argument. She nervously grinned and gave a small wave back.

"Why is she here?" Mike adjusted his tinted glasses on his nose.

"She's here to hear us rehearse the new set for the Bowl," Jesse said. They all adjusted and went to their stations. He gave her a smile, but she could tell it was forced.

She wanted to run out of there, but her feet felt like cement. This was so not the time and place for her to be there. She was an intruder on something personal and private and darn right unsettling. With arms crossed in front of her, she sat next to the soundboard, and the sound engineer adjusted their levels. As he did, the band started mumbling suggestions for a song list. Soon they warmed up a bit and focused on the work.

With the argument on pause for now, the tension in Charlotte's chest eased, allowing her to inspect the room. It was plain with the same orange-tinted wood paneling. A red and ebony Indian area rug was sprawled out on the floor, a couch was stuffed in a corner, and their instruments were hooked up to a few amplifiers. The room had history.

It was quite fascinating hearing them discuss their reasonings behind the show order, mostly to accommodate Danny's voice. Some songs were easier to sing, in turn giving him a vocal rest. Others had a natural transition into the next song. These details were new to her. After an hour or so, they nailed down a set list for a two-hour show and discussed individual solos to showcase everyone's talent. They worked through those transitions and composed some new introductions to a few of the songs to keep it fresh.

What seemed so trivial was actually more intricate, and she loved hearing every bit of it.

It hadn't gone unnoticed to Charlotte how casually they dressed. Some wore shorts, and others wore sweatpants and sneakers. They looked like normal guys. It was a contrast to their performance clothes and their posters and album covers. Here they were just regular guys, guys who mowed lawns or watched the football game on Sundays. They kind of reminded her of Jason's dad.

Charlotte had spent many Sundays with the Hunter family, listening to Mr. Hunter and his sons yell at the TV when a player fumbled a ball. Football was serious business in their house.

Mr. Hunter was a cool guy. He was awfully funny and proudly proclaimed himself as a joke machine. Without fail, he always made her laugh with the most awful jokes. When together, Jason and his brother, Timothy, bantered back and forth and had Charlotte on the floor. Those were good memories.

Charlotte blinked a few times, coming out of her thoughts. She wasn't back home with the Hunters. She was in a recording studio with six strangers. It was so surreal. It was like a scene from a movie, yet she didn't know how to act or how to play her part.

To her relief, the argument seemed long forgotten to the musicians but not to her. They were so vindictive, especially Jesse and Scott.

Jools and Madalen had hinted at it. Now, she heard it firsthand. Why was Jesse so adamant about making new music? Why would he want to risk Danny losing his voice or Reggie divorcing his wife? It didn't seem right, she hated to admit.

"Hey, Charlotte." Danny's voice pulled her out of her head. "You want to hear something brand new?"

She nodded eagerly.

Danny tapped his foot, and they all began with powerful a cappella harmonies. A shiver ran up her spine, and goosebumps went down her arms. After a dramatic pause, Roy entered with a fill on the toms, and Mike came in with the piano. The music was upbeat with a mysterious melody. Reggie provided movement with his bass. Roy played a melodic groove, and Danny's voice soared. The lyrics were haunting. A man walked alone through darkness. The first verse painted him in isolation. By the second verse, Danny sang of someone stepping into the shadows beside him. Both faced the darkness together and, in the end, they found the light.

After the bridge, Danny sustained a note, and Jesse seamlessly entered in with his guitar solo. Roy came in with triplicate fills, which brought Danny back in with the chorus. This time Roy hit the high hat to add extra height to the song as Danny repeated the chorus. Jesse and Scott's guitar playing grew intense as all their voices intertwined in rippling echoes of harmonies. Then they stopped abruptly, and all of them sang the last phrase.

Charlotte jumped to her feet with a standing ovation. Roy playfully bowed, and Reggie pretended to blush. "Oh, my gosh. That was so good. I loved every single second of it. The vocals. Roy, your drumming. Reggie, you killed it. You guys are amazing."

"Can we assume you'll give a favorable review in your article?" Reggie asked.

"Oh, my gosh, yes," Charlotte assured. She asked them a few questions about the song and how they wrote it, which led to her asking a few of the questions Jason had given her. "How do you guys go about writing an album? Is there some kind of format or concept to it?"

Scott put a hand to his chest. "We've intentionally stayed away from strict structuring or formatting. We don't want to put ourselves in a box."

"If you do that, then you become the generic pop crap on the radio that's a dime a dozen," Roy interjected.

Mike pushed his glasses up on his nose. "Sometimes it's hard to tell where we're going to go musically. We have six diverse individuals here. Sometimes it starts with a sound or melody. Then someone else might have their own interpretation on it, and it'll finish with a different spin."

Scott leaned forward. "All of us have ideas floating around in our heads, and then we flesh those ideas out."

Charlotte scribbled a flurry of notes. At one point she flicked her eyes to the side toward Jesse. She had grown accustomed to seeing him forever with a guitar. "What about the lyrics? Who writes those mainly?"

Danny's smooth voice answered, "Mike is a strong lyricist, and he and I hash it out. Sometimes I know what I want to say but can't put it into words, and so Mike and I work together to make it come across the right way."

Mike spoke up, "And Jesse's guitar playing enhances it by coming up with backing melodies."

Charlotte shot Jesse a quick look. He listened to the conversation but kept forming chords on the fretboard. A few more questions were asked, and they politely answered. Roy made a few jokes, and Reggie chimed in as a comedic duo. Wrapping up the interview with a few trivial questions, she asked about their favorite lyrics, chord progressions, and most important, what famous musicians had sung in this room.

Breaking for lunch, the sound engineer remained to reset their instruments.

Charlotte caught Roy at the door. "Roy, I wanted to ask you where do you think you'd be if music had been taken away in school?"

He crimped his lips with a stifled goofy expression. "Making holes in people's roofs."

Charlotte eyed him with a grin. "And your uncensored answer?"

He laughed. "Still a virgin."

Charlotte giggled and shook her head as they bumped fists and filtered out, except for Jesse. A second sound engineer, a woman, joined the first, and they worked quietly in the background. Whispers drifted from over the soundboard. Charlotte debated about following them out but also wanted to stick around. Should she talk to him or leave? Picking at her notebook, she thanked her brain for coming up with an idea.

"I have a confession."

He stopped mid-strum and met her gaze.

"I've never played the guitar."

He smiled. "Oh, yeah?"

She stepped into the center of the room. "I don't think I've even picked one up. Olivia, my friend, plays, but I've never tried. It always looked too hard."

"Nah, it's not too hard. Come here." Offering her a chair, he then removed the guitar from around his shoulder and handed it to her. He grabbed an acoustic guitar and put it on his lap. "Now, put your index finger on the first fret here on the B string, then your middle finger on the second fret of the D string. Then put your ring finger on the third fret of the A string." She listened to his instructions and mirrored his hand. "Now when you strum, don't strum the top string."

"All righty." She strummed.

"And that's a C chord. Now keep strumming it." He tapped his foot to the time he wanted her to strum, and she started. Strumming with her, he soon added riffs to complement the C chord.

"We made a song," she said gleefully, releasing her hand from the fret. "Can I learn another one?"

They spent the next ten minutes playing different chords and making up songs.

In the back of the taxi, Charlotte smiled so hard her cheeks hurt. Her heart swelled in her chest. He'd taken time out of his lunch break to teach her guitar. He was patient and a great teacher.

But as the city whizzed past the windows, her smile faded. That argument was awkward. Rock stars were known for tempers. She'd read enough entertainment magazines to know that. Yet hearing them actually lock horns unsettled her.

Maybe he just had a bad day? They were all tired. Even she could snap at Olivia or Jason toward the end of the school year. That didn't make her a bad person.

If he really was her father, she needed him to be steady more than driven. She needed him to be the man who laughed easily over pie and patiently taught a girl a few chords. That was the version Charlotte held onto, the only one she chose to believe in.

Opening the apartment door, she found her aunt sitting at the bar top with drink in hand. "Hi, Aunt Becky." She hung her purse on the hooks by the door.

"Hello." Her aunt's eyes narrowed. "You've been gone all morning."

"Yeah, sorry I'm later than I expected. Your hair, gosh it's so beautiful." Charlotte held a shiny lock of Aunt Becky's golden hair in her fingers. "They did a good job."

"You were out with Matt?"

Charlotte flopped on the couch. "Yep, we lost track of time."

"Why don't I believe you?" Becky slipped off the barstool and came around the couch with hands on her hips.

"Uh . . . what do you mean?"

"I mean Matt called just a few minutes ago and said he wasn't going to be able to hang with you for the next couple of days because of work."

"Oh." Her pulse quickened as her brain scrambled, coming up empty. "Umm."

"All right, missy." She waved a finger at her with a grin on her face. "You've been up to something, and I want to know what it is."

"I haven't been up to anything." Even she winced at how unconvincing it sounded.

Aunt Becky eyed her. "Come on. Fess up or I'll do something drastic."

Charlotte chuckled. "Drastic? Like what?"

"Like call your mom and tell her I don't know what you've been doing."

Charlotte shot forward. "Don't do that, please."

Aunt Becky laughed. "Oh, I wouldn't dream of it, but your reaction tells me you have been keeping something from me. Oh, come on. Tell me, or I'll just die." She pleaded like a toddler.

Charlotte fessed up with a laugh. "All right, all right. But you have to promise to keep it a secret."

"Ooh, it's juicy. I knew it." Aunt Becky leaned forward.

Charlotte explained about the article and that Caravan was the subject, further explaining Jason's involvement with backstage access, interviews with the band, and sitting in on a rehearsal.

Becky's mouth dropped, and her eyes bugged out. "You mean you've been talking in person to the members of one of the greatest rock 'n' roll groups of the '70s and '80s, and you kept this from me?!"

"Well, yeah."

Becky screamed like a teenager. "You've got to be kidding me, girl. How dare you keep a secret this monumental from me! I have been a major fan of theirs since their debut album. Oh, my gosh, you've been sitting on a powder keg."

"I guess it's a good thing that I have two tickets to their opening night at the Hollywood Bowl, including backstage access."

Becky screamed again. "This is fantastic. This is even better than what I had planned. That second ticket better be for me."

Charlotte reassured her through her giggles. "Yes. There's no one I'd rather go with."

"And I'll bring my camera. They might let me get some shots. Several of Danny Racer. Good grief. He's still gorgeous. Oh, this'll be great." Becky paced back and forth.

"They played me a new song they've never recorded before."

Aunt Becky stopped and sat on the coffee table across from her goddaughter. "You better tell me every little detail."

Charlotte clasped her hands to her chest. "It was something on another level. Their harmonies gave me chills, and I can't even begin to describe the music. It was fresh and new and exciting. Oh, Aunt Becky, it was incredible."

Aunt Becky playfully smacked the girl's knee. "I hate you."

Charlotte giggled. "Then I guess I'll see if Matt wants to go with me to their opening night."

"Not a chance. You bet your sweet britches I'm going," Aunt Becky said, pointing a warning finger at the girl. "And you're going to introduce me to them."

Charlotte grinned. "Deal."

"Oh! I have so much to do. We've got appointments to make and shopping to do."

"You just got your hair done."

"We've got to buy ourselves new dresses, shoes, the works." She read the time on her dainty wristwatch. "Come on, shopping first."

Charlotte laughed as she was practically dragged out of the apartment.

Chapter 12

Hollywood Bowl

The next week was spent shopping and attending theatrical performances. They went to Santa Monica beach for swimming, sunbathing, and collecting shells, and of course sightseeing at the Pier. Aunt Becky filled their time with laughter and fun. They experienced Fourth of July fireworks back at the beach and saw the new movie *Speed* at the movie theater. Charlotte introduced her aunt to grunge music, and they caught Caravan on Jay Leno's *Tonight Show* promoting their upcoming concert.

The morning of Caravan's concert, giddy like a toddler, Charlotte approached the outside landing at the Griffith Observatory. "The telescope." Charlotte pointed and ran to it. "I can't believe I'm actually here. Really here."

Rebel Without a Cause was hers and Olivia's comfort movie. Their friends thought it was weird because it's such a dramatic movie. Nothing *feel-good* about it. But to them, it was their go-to film.

When Olivia's uncle died unexpectedly, Charlotte didn't know how to be there for her friend. So she made some cookies, rented the VHS tape, and the two curled up in the basement and cried from the opening credits to the very last scene. Once the movie had finished, they were all cried out, and the cookie plate was empty.

"James Dean stood in this exact spot." Charlotte stood frozen, her hands splayed out beside her in dramatic fashion.

"What are you doing?"

"Soaking it in."

Aunt Becky threw her head back and laughed.

Over the next several minutes, she reenacted the knife fight scene for her aunt, spouting every line with supreme accuracy. "Olivia is totally going to flip."

Charlotte pretended to powder her nose with an imaginary compact and struck a pose as her aunt snapped another picture.

Putting a few coins into the telescope, they took turns peering through it to view the Hollywood Sign. Then Charlotte snatched her aunt's hand and dragged her to the front steps of the Observatory to find the spot where the movie came to an end. "I wish Olivia were here. She'd be screaming her head off. Who am I kidding? If she were here, I'd be screaming my head off."

"Lucky for my eardrums, she isn't." Her aunt chuckled. "We were the same for our idols back in the day."

From the parking lot shuttle to a taxi to Lake Hollywood Park, they took photos of the Hollywood Sign in the distance. Following Aunt Becky's suggestion, they hiked a path to Mount Lee Summit, getting closer to the sign for several great shots.

The mountainside was covered with trees that looked thirsty for water under the hot summer sun. These were entirely different sorts of mountains than she was used to. Charlotte's hometown had mountains. They were lush green peaks and valleys rich with color, even during the summer months, and a vibrant canvas painting of warm hues during the autumn season.

Their original plan of hiking up behind the sign was canceled because of their exhaustion. Hailing a taxi, they stopped at the film store to pick up Charlotte's developed film.

With the film store only a few blocks away from home, they chose to walk it despite their aching legs. Charlotte couldn't wait for the cold air conditioner. Her clothes were stuck to her body, and her feet grew heavier with each step. At the last intersection, a swarm of motorcyclists came to stop at the red light.

"Oooh, look at that one." Becky leaned in close as she pointed. "They must be part of some bike club." She then took it upon herself to approach the cute one.

"Aunt Becky!" Charlotte chided before reluctantly following. Who knew if she needed to keep her aunt from hopping on the back of one of the bikes.

"Where are you headed?" Becky asked with a dazzling smile.

The cute one answered, "We're taking a road trip to San Diego."

"Oh, that sounds like fun." Aunt Becky stepped closer. "Have room for one more?"

The light turned green, and Charlotte yanked her aunt away to the safety of the curb as the riders all revved their engines and rode off.

"What were you thinking?" Charlotte scolded. "Were you actually going to get on his bike?"

"No. But I might've gotten his phone number for the next road trip." Aunt Becky flicked back her sun-kissed hair.

"Why is it that I feel like the parent and you're the child."

"One time your mother and I met a few people at a diner who had a truck. They were headed to San Francisco for the weekend. They offered us a ride in the bed of their truck. And so we went."

"You went with total strangers?"

"We actually saw a few shows with them, and they drove us back."

"You and mom were crazy."

"We had fun. We watched drag racing, and your mom even participated in a race. She persuaded some guy to teach her how to ride his motorcycle and race it."

"Who *are* you?"

Aunt Becky threw back a laugh and guided them into the apartment building. After refreshing showers and changing clothes, they nestled onto the cloud couch and rifled through the photographs.

Becky loved the pictures of Charlotte with the band members and a few candid shots of them performing. She lifted one up, examining it closely. "This is framed really nice. Great composition. We have a budding photographer."

"I just pointed and shot. That was pure luck."

Aunt Becky held up the picture of Jesse and Charlotte. "You photograph well. Ever thought about being a model?"

Charlotte scrunched her face.

"He is just as sexy as he was back then. This man is aging like a fine wine." Aunt Becky flipped through the other pictures and stopped on the singer. "And then of course there's Mr. Danny Racer. Gorgeous eyes and face with hair that made every girl jealous. He was my favorite. Your mom and I would always debate who was sexier, Danny or Jesse. We made such fools of ourselves over it."

Charlotte perked up. "My mom, she liked Jesse?"

"Oh my, yes. She had such a thing for him." She glanced at her wristwatch. "We've got to start getting ready for the concert."

Charlotte couldn't believe how perfect Aunt Becky's apartment building was located. They were within walking distance of the amphitheater, and the crowd was already forming at the main gate. When it was their turn, they stepped up to the box office and gave their names. An usher appeared and escorted them down a narrow side alley along the stage.

Gripping her purse, Charlotte hoped she'd find the right moment to tell Jesse she was his daughter before their time ran out. This might be her last visit with him. It was the best time, the only time.

As they slipped behind the stage, Charlotte hugged her aunt really tight. "I can't believe this is happening. Oh, remember you're pretending to be my teacher."

"And explain again to me why I have to go along with this ruse?"

"I'm writing a paper. But I guess you could pretend to be my mom if you want?"

"I can't be your aunt?"

"I told Mr. Jackson my teacher was a huge fan."

Becky resigned with a wave. "Honey, I'll be whatever he wants me to be."

Charlotte's stomach fluttered as they approached a canvas tent tucked behind the stage. Crew members moved between road cases, cables, and sound equipment. The tent was small and plain—just folding chairs, a plastic table with bottled water, and a bench along one side. The smell of cigarette smoke hung in the air. She blinked. Was this it? No glamorous dressing room? It reminded her of their makeshift room at the Pier.

The canvas flap shifted and Danny stepped out first, grinning, his feathered hair tousled.

Gosh, he was gorgeous.

Charlotte winced as her fingers were crushed by her aunt.

"Hey, Charlotte. Come on in." Danny guided them inside. "It's Miss Charlotte Reynolds."

Scott and his wife, Nicole, lounged on folding chairs, while Mike and Jools were settled on a bench. Charlotte did a quick scan of the small space. Jesse wasn't there.

Charlotte thanked them again for the follow-up interview, then made a hasty introduction. "I hope it's all right. This is my teacher, Becky Thompson. She's been wanting to meet you. She's a real fan."

"Ah, the teacher for the article. Not a problem. Hi, Becky Thompson." Danny put out his hand.

Her aunt giggled and grew a shade of red. "I am suddenly at a loss for words," Becky stated.

"That's a first." Charlotte chuckled.

"Hey, it's Charlotte," Roy's booming voice bellowed as he blew into the tent and met her aunt/teacher. Jesse and Reggie followed behind, and soon the whole group gathered and made small talk. After Becky's initial shock of meeting her idols wore off, Charlotte had to admit her aunt did an impressive job of portraying a teacher, enthusiastic about the fine arts and their importance.

As the conversation continued, Charlotte eyed each band member intently from her perch on a folding chair. Her eyes darted from one member to the next. The tension from her last encounter with the band had vanished. No one distanced themselves or threw icy glares, only excited energy for the show. They must have forgiven or forgotten.

In a casual circle, Aunt Becky close to Danny, they reminisced about shows she'd attended years ago. Charlotte caught eyes with Jesse, who smiled warmly and nodded. In a few minutes, she would confess to him that she was his daughter. It was hard to swallow.

"Did you have any more questions for us, Charlotte?" Scott asked as he shifted in the folding chair.

Charlotte pulled her attention away from Jesse. "Um . . . yes." She fumbled for the notebook from her purse. With pencil in hand, she asked, "If you could say something to the schools who are fixing to take away the fine arts programs, what would you say?"

Scott rubbed his bottom lip. "Well, to me music is a form of expression and is needed for young people trying to find themselves. It allows them to be free. To feel something they've never felt before. I know it was that way for me. I wanted to create something new and exciting. It can be like reading a book and escaping to another land, creating stories and experiencing them firsthand. Keep music education in schools. That's a direct quote." He chuckled and she wrote it down.

"Hey, thanks." She glanced at her wristwatch, then to Jesse standing in the circle.

Reggie sat next to Jools on the bench and greeted the young journalist. "What's happening, Charlotte?"

Charlotte turned to him, a twinge of sadness tugged in her heart for his marital troubles. "Hey, Reggie. Can I ask you an additional question for the article?"

"Absolutely."

"So for those doubting music education as important, thinking students are learning nothing but sex, drugs, and rock 'n' roll still, what do you say to them?"

Reggie's expression widened. "Great question." He cleared his throat dramatically. "I'll tell you what schools will want to hear. While there is a freedom and a fun to creating music, there is also a sense of structure and discipline. A strong work ethic too. I think some might be forgetting this and only focusing on the glamorous aspect they deem dangerous or scary. If you're serious about music, you have to show up and put in the time and effort, and you'll be better for it. I think that's what the schools should focus on." He stood and gave a half bow, and Jools applauded playfully.

What did he say? Charlotte could barely focus on his answer. Time was slipping away. She scribbled as much as she could remember.

She had to do it—now. Maybe she could ask to talk off to the side. But springing it on him right before a show, was that really a good idea? Her stomach twisted, her thoughts spun, and a lump formed in her throat.

Aunt Becky took out her camera and asked if she could have one picture to capture this special moment. Everyone agreed, and they all clustered together in the small tent. Danny draped his arm over Aunt Becky's shoulder, and Jools took the photo for them.

Charlotte turned to Jesse beside her. "Can I . . . I mean, can I talk to you for a minute?"

His warm smile didn't ease her stomach. "Sure."

Just then, J. J. appeared, pushing aside the flap. "Time to head out, boys. Hey, Charlotte, nice to see you again." He extended his giant bear paw to Becky and made a brief introduction.

No, no! She needed more time. She had to tell him. But the band said their goodbyes and filed out. She stared after him. That was her chance. Her opportunity. And just like that, it was gone. What could she do?

"Thank you for letting me drool over your husbands," Aunt Becky said, formally thanking the wives.

They graciously understood. "Would you both like to watch the show with us?"

"Thank you, but we got tickets," Charlotte said, desperately fighting back tears threatening to surface. They had been so generous that she didn't want to take it for granted.

Collecting her purse, she stuffed her notebook inside, and pulled her aunt out of the tent, scanning the crew and stagehands for one last glimpse of him, her last bit of hope dwindling.

Jools followed them outside. "Charlotte, the boys have enjoyed their visits with you. You've made an impression on them."

"Really?" She snapped her attention back toward the wives filing out of the tent.

"We are having a party Monday evening as a celebration for one of their albums going double platinum. You both are welcome to attend. It's casual, and you can bring husbands or children."

Charlotte's mouth gaped open, hope shooting through her. "Thank you."

It was all she could say. Words couldn't express how she felt. She looked at Aunt Becky, eyes pleading.

"That is a very thoughtful invitation. We'd love to go," her aunt said.

Charlotte scribbled down the address and time.

"We hope to see you there," Nicole stated as she and Jools went off to find their places.

"Did we just get invited to a party at Mike Tennet's house?" Aunt Becky whispered, "I'm going to Mike Tennet's house. I'm cool. I'm good." She squeezed Charlotte's arm to contain an explosion of emotion. Once it passed, she wrapped her arm around her goddaughter. "Have I told you how wonderful it is to have you here this summer?"

They found their seats outside in the open auditorium on the right side of the stage. Jesse's side. The iconic dome-shaped shell was a thrilling sight. Seeing the lighting rigs, the equipment, and the sold-out crowd was something she'd only read about with past legends who had played at the outdoor venue. Experiencing it now was so surreal that she discreetly pinched herself.

The drums started with an up-tempo beat, and the lights pulsated to Roy's timing. Next came the guitars as the whole audience started clapping to the beat. Danny raced on stage to thunderous applause.

He grabbed the microphone and started to sing "King of Fools." It was a rocky and energetic song with a driving rhythm. Jesse played a wicked guitar solo, which sent the audience into hysterics.

From the very first song, Aunt Becky had become her younger self. Whisked to her feet, Charlotte was sucked into the energy of the crowd. It was electrifying. They danced with the people next to them and sang at the tops of their lungs. Many times, Aunt Becky and Charlotte burst into fits of laughter. This concert was so much more than the little show they did at the Pier. For two hours, Danny never stopped moving. He kept the energy of the crowd alive as he jumped and raced around the stage.

About halfway through the concert, Charlotte had a realization. This was a small taste of what the '70s and '80s must have felt like for her mom and Aunt Becky. It was the closest she would ever come to stepping into her mother's past.

She looked up at Jesse the way her mom once must have, from the crowd. Both of them watched the same man who seemed larger than life under the lights.

A few times Jesse caught her in the crowd and grinned. At one point, he tossed his pick in her direction. She reached for it, but someone else was quicker. She shrugged back at him.

Without warning, a surge of emotion swelled within her. Tears rolled down her cheeks even as she smiled from ear to ear. Maybe it was pride. Maybe it was something deeper. Whatever it was, seeing him on stage, feeling him see her, was unlike anything she'd ever known.

He had to be her father. He just had to.

The two shut the door to the apartment, their chests still pounding and bodies trembling. Aunt Becky sank into the couch and winced as she slipped off her flats and rubbed her feet. "That was the best night, a night like I haven't had in several years. They can still put on the most fantastic show. I feel drunk."

"I kind of feel that way too." Even though she'd never gotten drunk, Charlotte squished into the comfy cushions. With a groan, she propped her sore legs up on the coffee table and wriggled her toes.

"It was as if I was transported back in time to the '70s, back when we were young." Aunt Becky poured herself a glass of brandy, then sank back down next to her goddaughter. "What a magical night."

"I wouldn't mind if we went again. And again and again." Charlotte giggled.

"You want to see them *again*?"

Charlotte squeezed a pillow to her chest and nodded.

"I'd certainly love to see that show at least one more time. I will see what kind of pull I have. Maybe my boss can snag a couple of tickets. That's what we did back in the day. We went to many shows over and over to relive the same experiences and make new memories."

"So, you and my mom liked them a lot."

Aunt Becky nodded emphatically from behind the rim of her glass. "Oh my, yes. We went to many, many concerts. We were massive fans of Caravan. We had backstage passes and everything. We faked a few of them."

"You could do that?"

"It was easier to do back then. We met them several times. Hold on a moment." Moving stiffly, she rose and retrieved a thick photo album from a closet. She placed it down on the coffee table, and they sat on the floor. "This is our photo album from back then. We took so many pictures, but I kept the albums with me so your mom's parents never saw what we did. They were a bit stricter than my parents."

It was Charlotte's turn to be jealous. She inspected every single photograph of her mom and aunt next to different famous rock stars. Her mom was young and beautiful. Wearing flared jeans and halter tops, her long billowy auburn hair flowed past her shoulders. In these old photographs, her mom glowed with a kind of carefree happiness.

Her eyes stopped on a picture of Aunt Becky and her mom with Caravan. "That's them," she exclaimed.

"Yep. All six. Big haired vessels of gorgeousness."

In another picture, her mom stood next to Jesse with his arm fixed around her waist. Inspecting all the other pictures, she saw one of her aunt and her mom kissing Jesse on either cheek at the same time.

Aunt Becky laughed. "I forgot about that. He was so nice. We were such crazy fans. Would've done anything for them."

Charlotte glanced up at her aunt after finding a picture of her aunt locking lips with Danny. "Would've done anything, huh?"

"They were more casual back then." She cleared her throat. "I think that was at an after-party or something."

Charlotte flipped through every picture. There were shots of different bands performing on stage and snapshots of the girls posing with rockers: Robert Plant, Sammy Hagar, Styx, Paul Rodgers, Steve Perry, Neal Schon, and Gregg Rolie, to name a few.

"We kind of got around."

"I can see." Charlotte chuckled. "This is incredible."

Her aunt brought these memories to life with story after story, but her voice faded away when Charlotte caught sight of another picture of her aunt posing with Danny. At first glance, it was nothing, but in the background, Charlotte spotted her mother passionately kissing Jesse on the lips.

Then her aunt said, "Lori was a bit of a wild one back then. Flashed the musicians, partied, that sort of thing. Don't tell her I blabbed. We went to so many concerts. But that's what you did. You went to have a good time. And Jesse was something back then too." She pointed to a picture of Jesse with her. "He wore really tight pants."

"Aunt Becky," she groaned.

Chapter 13

Invitation

Charlotte tossed and turned all night. Her mind spun endlessly, rehashing everything her aunt had divulged. As morning came, bright pink and gold sunlight peeked over the sleepy horizon. It was beautiful, but it didn't compare to her sunrises back home. Sitting on the cozy front porch of her fairy-tale house as the vibrant sun rays stretched over the treetops was magical.

Finally with a sigh, she threw aside the sheets and went out onto the balcony with her notebook and pencil to sketch, but not before she grabbed a chocolate chip muffin from the kitchen counter.

The evidence piled up, and it was more and more clear. Jesse Holt was her father. No one could refute his name on her birth certificate. Maybe her mother got pregnant and didn't tell him about his child because of his lifestyle? That could be possible. It would explain why Jesse wasn't a part of her life. Maybe he hadn't been given the choice. But why did her mom vehemently refuse to even touch the topic?

The distant noise of cars and street sounds disrupted her thoughts a few times as she started to draw the body of a guitar. She was used to songbirds or a robin to quiet her mind, but the city sounds would have to do.

Jesse Holt's age was about right. He would've been young, but twenty-two wasn't too young, especially at the height of his success and popularity. It would have been easy for him to father a child with her nineteen-year-old mother.

Then there were the confessions from her aunt's own lips. Her mom had a thing for the guitarist, and they had constant debates over who was cuter—the singer or the guitarist. And to top it all off, there were countless pictures of them kissing or arm in arm. They were more than friendly. Charlotte scrunched her nose at the idea. If it wasn't a relationship, then maybe a one-night stand, ending with her mom deciding to raise the baby by herself.

Of course, Charlotte couldn't forget all the similarities: She was left-handed like him, and his grandma's name was Charlotte. They had the same big smile and big teeth, not to mention the one dimple on the same side. Jason and even Aunt Becky had agreed they looked similar. Then they both liked the same flavor of pie. This was more of a coincidence, admittedly, but still boysenberry was pretty rare.

Jesse Holt was her father. She blew out a puff of air. She'd found her father. The person she'd wanted to find all her life was alive. So close. So real.

Charlotte popped a piece of chocolate chip muffin into her mouth and savored the flavor. They had bought some from the store earlier in the week. Homemade was better, but it at least satisfied her craving.

Charlotte added details to the tuning keys on her paper. Her brow furrowed, still confused as to the reason for her mom's secrecy. By now, she was old enough to know the truth and to understand. It didn't make any sense why her mom held fast to this secret.

A twinge of frustration bubbled up, and she pressed the pencil harder onto the page. This whole time she'd been out on the Coast, the gnawing in her stomach had nearly gone. That hollow sensation of uncertainty about herself hadn't seemed to haunt her like it did at home. She'd almost forgotten what it felt like.

Now here it was in full force, the questions, the uncertainty, the fluttering of butterflies. And who was to blame for it all? Her mom. Her mom's determination to keep this secret made life unbearable sometimes. And how dare she distance herself and leave her alone without another parent to turn to. Not knowing her father hadn't just left a gaping hole in her life, it kept her from understanding many parts of herself.

One thing was for sure; her mom's selfishness wasn't going to stop her. She wanted answers, and she'd get them. She refused to feel worthless anymore.

As Charlotte leaned forward to add more detail to the penciled fingers on the neck of the guitar, a thought came to her. Was there a falling out? Had the last time they'd been together ended in a huge fight? Maybe her mom was angry at him? That might explain not wanting to talk about it. But the idea of her mom holding a grudge for all these years didn't seem right.

Maybe it was unrequited love? Had her mom been longing for him all these years? And was it painful? Or maybe they were two lost souls pulled apart by circumstance? A famous rock star and a small-town girl in the crowd. That kind of story didn't usually end well.

With her pencil between her lips, a small smile formed. If she could reunite them, maybe it could end differently. Maybe they could finally be a family. It'd change everything.

Charlotte finished shading the sunglasses on her paper. After a moment, she analyzed the drawing. It was Jesse playing the guitar. Brushing her representation of him with her fingers, she grinned fondly.

The sky was brighter over the cityscape, and the heat seeped into her skin. Charlotte finished her muffin and drank her juice, trying to quiet down the flittering inside her stomach. She didn't know how she'd do it yet, but this summer she would reunite her family, and life would finally make sense. This was happening.

Charlotte closed her notebook, went inside, and put her dishes in the sink.

The phone rang and she snatched it on its first ring, not wanting to wake her aunt. "Thompson residence."

"Morning, Charlotte."

"Hi, Mom." Charlotte sank into the couch.

"How are you? You having fun?"

"Yep." She glanced at the clock. It was almost noon back home. Her mom should've been showing a house to a client or something.

"That's good. I got your postcards. I have them up on the fridge. Grandma saw them and, in her roundabout way, said she wants a postcard from you. You might send one to her."

"I'll pop one in the mail."

"What new and exciting things have you done?"

Charlotte propped her feet on the coffee table. "Did you get the postcards about the fireworks on the beach and the pictures of the Hollywood Sign?"

"Yes. They are wonderful. I can't believe you saw Meryl Streep at Chasen's. I like her movies." Her mom sounded genuinely impressed. "Kind of reminds me of what Aunt Becky and I used to do when we were your age."

"Among other things," Charlotte muttered.

"What was that?"

"Oh, nothing."

"What else have you done?"

"Most recently we went to the Griffith Observatory."

"Oh, I bet Olivia will be excited to hear about that."

She'd also been hanging out with her father who her mom never told her about.

"Is Aunt Becky still staying out of trouble?"

"Yeah. She's been good."

"I'm glad." Lori laughed, then continued on, "Oh, I ran into Matt's mom at the grocery store. I told her how he's been so nice to you out there. We talked about how quiet he was at the church potlucks. I remember receiving only a grunt or a nod from him. Interesting kid."

"Interesting adult," Charlotte said.

"She was happy he's found the time to show you around. He usually throws himself into his work."

Charlotte frowned. "Are you checking up on me?"

"No. Just making conversation."

"He's been very nice," Charlotte said with a snipped tone.

An awkward silence hung between them. Charlotte stared at the entertainment unit, then exhaled. "I have so many pictures to show you when I get back."

This appeased her mom. "I can't wait to see them and you. It's gotten quite lonely in this big old house. Enjoy the rest of your day. Tell Becky hi. Bye now."

"Bye." Charlotte hung up the phone, puzzled. Back home, her mom was always too busy with showings and clients, yet now, she miraculously found time to call and ask questions. To take interest. Charlotte stared at the phone. It was almost like her mom wished she was out here too.

Throughout the morning, Charlotte and Aunt Becky played a few card games, snacked on junk food, and sipped on Coke. Her parents and the nature of their relationship never left her mind. Many ideas on how to reunite them played out in her head.

She had seen movies where kids secretly plotted to put their parents in the same room together. That never seemed fair. This involved real emotions, including her own, so she decided to start carefully—tell him the truth first, gauge his reaction, and then work to get the two of them back together.

Their lazy afternoon involved a romantic comedy on the television. During the commercial, Aunt Becky pried herself off the couch to go to the restroom.

The phone rang.

Charlotte sprang up from her spot on the floor and snatched the receiver. "Hello? Thompson residence."

"Oh. Uh . . . hi, is this Charlotte Reynolds?"

"Yep. That's me."

"I thought that was you. It's Jesse . . . Holt."

Charlotte's mouth gaped open. The other side of the line was silent.

"Are you still there?"

Charlotte cleared her throat and pinched her arm to keep herself in check. "Yep. Still here. Just surprised to be talking to you."

"I remembered where I dropped you off and found your teacher's number. I was going to call her to ask for your number. Lucky you picked up."

"Uh . . . yeah. Um, I'm staying with her for a few days. She and my mom are good friends. Why'd you want my number? Are you wanting an exclusive or something?" she teased.

He chuckled. "No, no. Nothing like that. I'm calling because I have two extra tickets to see The Three Tenors concert this Saturday."

Was he inviting her to a concert? To spend time with her? He wouldn't do this for just anybody. Right? He must feel something for her. Her dad liked her. Twisting the skin on her arm, she said, "Oh, wow. You don't want to take your family or something? I'd feel bad swiping one of their seats." The pain from her arm kept her mouth from rambling.

He laughed. "No. My mom and dad have other plans, and my brothers turned me down."

"Their loss."

"Thank you."

"Why not. Sure. I'd love to go. What band is it?"

He laughed again. "It's not a band. It's opera."

Charlotte made an involuntary ick noise.

"Hey, you're judging it before you give it a chance. Since we talked about you not listening to much opera, I thought it'd be a great chance to check it out. You can say no, but if you and your mom want to come along, I have two extra tickets."

She definitely wanted to spend more time with him, but the idea of opera—it was a major turnoff. "Thank you for the invitation. Can I think about it and get back with you?"

"Sure. No sweat."

"Can I ask for your number? Is that something I can do? You being a celebrity and all."

"I don't hand it out for just anybody."

"I'll destroy all evidence."

"I can always count on you Agent Reynolds."

Charlotte grinned from ear to ear as she wrote down his number, then hung up the phone.

Her aunt came back into the room fluffing her hair. "Who was that, dear?"

"Jesse Holt."

Aunt Becky stopped right in her tracks, one foot suspended in the air. She teetered and caught herself before stumbling. "Girl, you better not be playing with me."

"I would never." Charlotte concealed the note with his number on it. She had to protect him from Aunt Becky.

"Why was he calling my number? What did he want? Tell me every little detail." Aunt Becky sat eagerly on the sofa.

"He is inviting me to some opera concert on the sixteenth."

Aunt Becky's eyes widened, and she snatched the teen's arm. "You mean he has tickets to The Three Tenors concert, and he's inviting you?"

"Yeah, it's nice and all, but it's opera."

"Oh, honey, you don't understand. This is the show of all shows. This is going to be broadcast across the world. It's José Carreras, Plácido Domingo, and Luciano Pavarotti backed by the Philharmonic. Tickets have been sold out. I wanted to take you but couldn't get any tickets."

Charlotte pursed her lips. "He did say I could bring my mom."

"He has three tickets? We've got to go. Wait a minute. You didn't say no? I'll smack you upside the head if you did."

"I said I'd think about it."

"What's there to think about? You're going. We're going. I'm not missing out on this show. You get him on the phone and tell him we are going."

Charlotte dropped her head back dramatically and groaned. "Fine."

Aunt Becky squealed. "Oh, my gosh, I can't believe it. He must have taken a shine to you, inviting you to a sold-out show."

"A while ago we talked about how I think opera is boring, but he likes it for some reason."

Aunt Becky squished into the couch. "A gorgeous man with culture. I like him more and more."

"Aunt Becky, try not to slobber all over your nice white couch." Charlotte teased as she grabbed the phone to dial.

Saturday evening came and even though she dreaded sitting through a snore fest, spending more time with Jesse was exciting. He had personally invited her. They made up an excuse as to why her teacher would be taking her mom's place.

Charlotte wore the formal dress she wore to Chasen's restaurant. Her hair was pinned up in a simple updo. Aunt Becky wore an elegant mid-length cream dress with gold designs on the sides and matching cream shoes and purse. She was beautiful.

A knock on the door.

Charlotte could hardly contain herself and briskly opened the door. There he was, standing in a fitted black suit and tie. While he looked handsome, it was odd seeing him so dressed up. "You look different," she blurted out.

"Thanks, I guess."

She scrunched her face. "Sorry. You look nice. Won't you come in? She's almost ready."

"Thanks." He took a few steps inside and stood in the entryway. Jesse Holt was in her apartment.

It was hard to take her eyes off him. Ever since hearing those stories and seeing the pictures of him and her mom, it was like viewing him in a whole different light. Not a celebrity or musician, but as her father.

"I'm beginning to believe your mom doesn't exist," he teased.

"Yeah, sometimes it feels that way. She's been busy with her work. But she hopes we have a good time and thanks you for this opportunity."

One of these days, Charlotte would bring them together in the flesh. It was only a matter of time. "How did you come by three tickets to an apparently sold-out show? Planned on taking a date or your mom?"

"No. Nothing like that. It was more something my grandmother listened to. I listen to it and like it because of her."

"Mr. Jackson let you play hooky from your concerts?"

"J. J.'s known about my having these tickets before scheduling the concert. Besides, everyone, and I mean everyone, will be tuning in to the opera tonight."

Aunt Becky appeared in the doorframe, striking a dramatic pose. "Don't I look absolutely breathtaking?"

Charlotte shook her head, a little embarrassed, as Jesse just chuckled. "Yes. Can we go now?"

Aunt Becky exhaled and sauntered over to the musician, draping a hand over his shoulder. "Honey," she tossed back to her goddaughter. "I wasn't asking you."

Jesse confirmed Charlotte's comment as he gave her his arm. "You look stunning."

A chauffeured limousine drove them to Dodger Stadium, gliding past miles of crawling freeway traffic bound for the same destination. As horns blared and brake lights flickered, their driver veered into a separate entrance, joining a quiet, orderly line reserved for VIP arrivals.

Charlotte shot forward in her seat when Tom Cruise stepped out of the limousine in front of theirs. With relentless excitement she tapped Aunt Becky's knee. "Oh my gosh! Oh my gosh! Oh my gosh! Do you see who that is? I loved his movie *A Few Good Men*!"

This didn't feel real.

Moments later, their doors opened, and they were ushered from their car. Once inside, an attendant led them down to the floor seats, Aunt Becky crushed Charlotte's fingers, her composure almost cracking. Seeing the sea of people and the massive stage before her, even Charlotte couldn't deny this was something special.

Charlotte sat in between Jesse and her aunt, allowing her to talk more with him about his grandmother and how many other operas he had been to. Apparently, his grandmother sang arias in the kitchen while making bread and pasta and beautiful lullabies while putting him to bed when he was a kid. "When I told her I was making rock 'n' roll music, she smacked me upside the head. Telling me it wasn't music. But I think she came around after a while. She'd come to many of our shows and knew a lot of our songs."

Charlotte couldn't get enough of him and was a bit disappointed when the lights dimmed and a hush swept through the crowd. If only they could continue talking. The first part of the concert was a bit blah, reminding her of the stiff societal luncheons back home. But she sat up straight and remained polite, resisting the urge to prop her chin on her hand.

As the opera unfolded, something happened. A quiet energy pulsated through the crowd and through her. It was different from her father's show, more subtle, but still electrifying, as if thousands of people were holding their breaths.

With each song, she inched forward, her elbows on her knees. Halfway through the concert, the singer, Pavarotti, sang a song called "Nessun Dorma." The full-piece orchestra, along with the audience, hung on his every word, his every breath. The music swelled, growing more full and more powerful. His voice reached a new intensive height.

Without any warning, she burst into tears as he held his last note, and the crowd erupted into applause. Still crying and blubbering, she shot to her feet along with everyone to give a standing ovation. Her head buzzed. Her mind felt numb. Her eyes filled with tears. But she wasn't sad. She wasn't completely happy either. She couldn't explain it. His voice. The music. It produced a wide range of emotions within her, emotions that bubbled up and came out through tears.

Wiping her eyes, she looked up to find Jesse smiling, his arm pulling her into a side hug. Through her blurry vision, she saw the music had affected him too.

After the concert, the thunderous applause softened into fifty thousand murmuring voices as the house lights came up.

"That was simply amazing. I am completely stunned. I have no words," Aunt Becky said, marveling at the show.

Jesse turned to Charlotte. "What do you think of opera now?"

Charlotte's head still buzzed. "Surprising. Being present with an audience and hearing it live takes on a whole new meaning. You have changed my mind."

He bowed dramatically.

"Thank you for inviting me. For us."

"You are welcome."

"We appreciate your generosity," Aunt Becky stated as they exited the aisles. "If someone told my seventeen-year-old self that many years later I would be going to an opera with Jesse Holt, I wouldn't have believed them."

Charlotte watched Jesse give a card to a staff member with their vehicle number on it. The staff member disappeared to dispatch their car, and Jesse led them into the stadium's lower-level tunnels. Security was tight as celebrities and VIPs were escorted through separate exits to private cars rather than to public pickup. The whole thing moved fast, and the quiet sense of urgency pressed in on Charlotte.

Jesse didn't seem bothered. He walked with ease, as if comfortable in a world she was still trying to understand. Her aunt took her hand and said to Jesse, "I remember those after-parties—well, parts of them. Charlotte's mom was a devoted fan. As best friends, we went to many of your shows together. The other night, I was telling Charlotte just how much of a fan her mom was and showed her pictures of us with you all."

"You can stop there," Charlotte interjected, afraid her aunt would ruin everything she had carefully crafted. When they arrived at the pickup point, their limousine pulled up as if by some coordinated magic. The car door was opened for them, and they slid inside. When the door shut, Charlotte could finally breathe away the press of the crowd.

"It sure was a different feeling back then," Aunt Becky said as she sat next to her goddaughter.

Jesse agreed, "I don't think it'll ever be like that again."

"The people, the crowds, the parties—"

"Can I please have details?" Both exchanged hesitant glances, and Charlotte raised an eyebrow. "Do I want details?"

"In this instance, the less you know the better," Aunt Becky said, patting the teen's hand.

Charlotte giggled and shook her head. "Can you imagine, I'm close to the age you and my mom were when you were doing some of the things you won't tell me about."

"Oh, don't say that." Her aunt brought her palm to her cheek. "And for the sake of your mom and me, don't ever do what we did."

"You don't want me to have a wild rebellious time in my life?"

"No," Jesse spoke up for the first time in his seat across from them. "At least not like anything we did."

"Here. Here," Aunt Becky concluded.

"You stay as you are." He flashed a bright smile.

"But that's not fun," Charlotte teased, and they were whisked back to their apartment.

Late into the night, Charlotte sprawled across her bed, writing in her notebook. She tried to capture every memory, every feeling. She wanted to hold onto all of it. Could she ever admit to Olivia that she enjoyed opera? Never in a million years.

Jesse surprised her. So did his invitation and opera. Somehow, it felt like he knew her in a way no one else did. Maybe it was fate, quietly aligning moments just to keep bringing them together.

Flipping through the photo albums again, she stared at a picture of him with his arm around her mother. He was becoming more than she could have ever imagined. More than just a rock star. Maybe, just maybe, he could be the father she'd always been waiting for.

Chapter 14

The Party

The night of the party at Mike's house couldn't come fast enough. Charlotte still couldn't believe they were going to celebrate along with the band receiving their double platinum album. Many big, important people were sure to be there with a lot of other famous musicians.

The taxi drove up a long driveway and dropped Charlotte and Aunt Becky off at the front of the large house. They were greeted by Jools, who played the graceful hostess. She gave a quick tour of the place for essentials like the bathroom and then food and drinks. The house was packed. Music blasted on the stereo, and children ran throughout the house.

Aunt Becky recognized several singers from her adolescence and vanished into the crowd to meet her idols. Charlotte spotted a few famous people in conversation but held back from bothering them. Instead, she grabbed a Coke and ate a few finger foods from the glamorous table.

"Hey, Charlotte." She turned to the loud gravelly voice resonating over the noise.

"Hey, Roy." She fist bumped his knuckles and sipped from her can.

"Glad you could make it."

"Congratulations on your album going double platinum. You guys deserve it."

He pretended to blush as he grabbed a drink from the table in front of them.

"Someday you'll make it into the Rock & Roll Hall of Fame." She raised her voice over the noise.

Danny appeared and reached in front of Roy for the chip bowl. "Charlotte, nice to see you."

Her heart fluttered at his closeness, and her palms instantly became sweaty. He smelled so good. "Hi." Why did he have to be so dreamy? This was ridiculous. At the same time, she knew she'd have the same kind of teenage girl crush on Johnny Depp if he was standing right in front of her.

"What are you two talking about?"

"She wants us to get into the Rock & Roll Hall of Fame," Roy said, then took a sip.

Danny shrugged. "Eh, it doesn't matter if we do or not."

Charlotte choked on her drink. "What? It's like only the greatest honor a rock 'n' roll band could get."

Danny and Roy exchanged amused glances.

"Your faith in us is the most important part. It's more about making records and the fans, not awards and whether or not we get into some hall of fame," Danny said.

Charlotte could not understand the singer's opinion. "On behalf of all fans, we'd love to see you get that recognition."

Roy puffed out his chest as he put his arm around her shoulder. "Yeah. Take that. I like her, Danny. Can we keep her?"

As other guests whisked Danny away, she chatted with Roy a little more about his upbringing, influences, and what he did in his down time. He wasn't married but had a girlfriend who was somewhere in the crowd. His praise for his parents warmed her heart.

Roy called over his pop and made introductions. Through their conversation, she learned that several other proud parents were at the party for their successful sons. His attention was appreciated because it was obvious there weren't any kids her age at this party. The oldest was ten or eleven.

"Are Jesse's parents here?" she asked innocently while finishing her drink.

Roy craned his tall frame over the crowd, then waved. "Eh, they're somewhere around here." Inevitably, Roy was swept away, and she was left to observe the party alone.

Her attention turned to the interior of the house, the house of a rock 'n' roll star. It was interesting, modern with touches of weird and exotic art and uniquely designed furnishings—way different from the quaint colonial cottages back home. She wasn't sure she understood it or even liked it.

Charlotte turned as collective cheers and laughter rang out. Someone must have been telling a particularly funny story. She craned her neck and spotted her aunt as part of the noisy crowd. Throughout the night, she glimpsed Jesse a few times, but he was always engaged in conversation. At one point, he stood beside a man who looked remarkably like him. Could that be his father? And was his mother somewhere in the kitchen? She half hoped to get a chance to talk with him some more but didn't want to monopolize his time.

The band was recognized for their accomplishment, and a few speeches were given. Then all six stood together with their framed albums, along with some of the executives from their label and, of course, their bear-like manager. Several photographs were taken, and Aunt Becky was among the photographers.

As the clock struck ten o'clock, the party took on a grown-up feel. The kids had ventured off to entertain themselves, and she was out of her element. The noise. The music. Her brain buzzed, and her head ached. She needed a break.

Grabbing a cookie, Charlotte found an escape through the sliding back door that led to the patio. The backyard was beautifully lit with a pool off in the back corner. Shutting the door helped muffle the noise, a relief to her eardrums. She bit off a hunk of cookie and sat on a lounge chair, staring mindlessly up at the sky.

Was this a taste of the lifestyle her mom lived? Noise. Chaos.

Partying. It overwhelmed Charlotte. How did her mom do this at seventeen?

Charlotte strained to see any of the constellations.

The party noise poured out onto the patio as the sliding door opened but was muffled again as the door was closed. She turned. Jesse stood on the step with a drink in his hand. Her insides did somersaults. "You escaping too?"

He eagerly joined her on the opposite lounge chair. "Man, I love him to death, but Dave Saunters, one of our executive producers from our label, tells the same stories over and over again. Must be the hundredth time I've heard his story about the time he and Eddie Walsh, the other bigwig, were stuck in a john with Sammy Hagar." He rolled his glass in his fingers. "What are you doing out here? You okay?"

"I'm all right. Just trying to see the stars. They're much brighter in my hometown."

"Are you getting a little homesick?"

It felt like she'd been smacked in the face with a bucket of ice water. Is that what she'd been feeling lately? A longing for home? "Hmm. I guess so."

"The glitz and glam has worn off. You start comparing everything as an ache grows in your gut?"

"You hit the nail on the head."

"Believe me, I know homesick. Years of being far from home makes you miss your stuff and hate hotel food."

"This party. It's put things into perspective."

"What do you mean?"

"This kind of lifestyle, night after night, day after day. How did you all do it back then?"

Jesse leaned back in his chair. "We were much younger."

"I know I joked the other night about it, but I don't think I could do it."

"Good. That gives me some relief."

"Relief? How so?"

"I don't know. I guess I've grown a little fond of you. I never had kids of my own, so I fall into the role of mentor sometimes. Don't want to see you make the wrong choices."

Charlotte blushed. "Jesse Holt taking a shine to me. I feel honored." They were quiet for a bit. "Did you always know you wanted to be a musician? Like was there something in you deep down that just knew this is what you're going to be or meant to be?"

Jesse scratched his head with a far-off look aimed at the pool. "I think I was influenced at a young age. My dad and grandfather were in the music industry. My grandmother constantly sang. I was surrounded by music all the time."

"So it was a family thing?"

"Sort of. I'm sure my parents would've supported me if I chose to go in a different direction. But once I picked up a guitar, I just knew."

"Was that when you were around ten?"

"You remember," Jesse said.

Charlotte slouched. It was so easy for everyone except her. "And that's who you are. A musician. You've always known."

He eyed her. "What do you want to be when you graduate?"

Charlotte threw up her hands. "I'm trying to figure that out. Lately, I feel stuck knee-deep in mud. Like I'm supposed to know but I don't."

"It'll come. Don't worry about it."

Charlotte let out a long, weary sigh. "Easier said than done."

They nodded hello to a couple strolling by and smiled at a few kids darting in and out of the house. When the ice clinked in his glass, she turned. He'd had a few drinks already. Was this a good time to ask a few sensitive questions? Maybe lowered inhibitions made honesty easier. "I have a confession to make."

"Another one?"

"I may have heard some of the discussion you all had in the rehearsal studio."

His back stiffened, and he looked down at his melting ice. "I'm sorry you heard that. We butt heads a lot, but that's just our way."

"I'm not taking sides or anything, but can I ask, why are you pushing the band to make more music and go out on tour again?"

He rolled the ice around in his empty glass.

"You can totally tell me to butt out. My best friend, Jason, does it all the time."

"As much as we love what we do, it is also our job. And a competitive one. We have to continue to work at it to stay on top."

She crimped her lips.

"What?" he asked.

"Nothing."

"No, you have something you want to say. You can say it."

"I mean no disrespect, but I find your answer hard to believe. Or at least not the only reason. The way you all were arguing—it's something you feel strongly about. Something other than Scott obviously feeling a little threatened by you."

Jesse rolled his eyes. "He's a jerk."

"It's more than a competitive job. There's something else. What is it?" Charlotte hoped she didn't upset him.

He heaved a sigh and stood, walking a few steps to nowhere in particular.

Did she anger him? Her fingers trembled, and a ball formed in her throat. She attempted to swallow it down, but it was stubborn. She was about to apologize for overstepping, but he spoke first.

"You may be right." His voice was quiet.

She froze. She was right? Whoa. There was something else. What was it? Many more questions flew past, but she bit the inside of her cheek to keep from spilling her guts.

They stood in silence.

Jesse shook his head. "I don't know. It's all becoming so confusing lately. Recently, I think . . . I feel like I'm chasing after something."

Charlotte came to his side. "What?"

He shuffled his feet. "I'm not sure." He looked down at his cup. "That's not true. It's like I have this obsession with the next show. The next performance. The next high. I need it."

"Why?"

He shifted his weight, struggling to come to grips with the truth.

"Because when I'm not up there on stage, it becomes very apparent how alone I am."

Charlotte's eyes widened. He feels alone? He's missing something—a family perhaps?

He scrubbed his face with his hand. "All these years, there's been nothing better than playing live, the anticipation, the exhilaration. There's something electrifying when you're up there and you connect with a crowd. And once you get it, you have to have more. It's like a drug." He shook his head. "And I think I've been addicted to it for so long that I've sacrificed the other part of my life. The part where I find someone to share it with."

Charlotte's throat tightened, and her voice cracked. "You'll—" She cleared her throat and tried again. "You'll find someone."

He drained the last watered-down droplets from the bottom of his glass and set it on the side table. "I'm pushing forty, and I have no one. Long ago, I had the opportunity to have a family, but I let it slip away." His gaze drifted. "And every year, I see the band growing further and further apart. The brotherhood is drying up. I'm trying desperately to hold onto something. I don't know."

Silence.

His voice was quiet as he let out a humorless chuckle. "Maybe Mike and Scott were right. Don't tell them that."

Charlotte offered a faint smile. "I know you didn't ask for my two cents, but I don't think you guys should go out on the road all angry with one another."

"Oh, that's nothing," he said easily. "We've done it for years."

"Though," she said, "it'd be a shame if the world didn't hear the amazing song you all performed the other day."

He looked down at the beginning stages of a crack in the pavement. "Don't take much stock, Charlotte, in not knowing what you want to be when you grow up. I knew exactly what I wanted." He paused and exhaled, then continued, "And it appears to have been my undoing—so to speak."

The words burned on her tongue. I'm your daughter. I'm right here. But she stayed silent. For some unknown reason, her gut told her it wasn't the time.

He tried to laugh. "Man, what a night. You get to hear the sob stories from a self-centered old man. Probably not what you expected when you came to this party." He forced a grin. "I'll let you get back to your teacher and the party. I don't think I'll be much company." He gave her arm an affectionate squeeze. "Night, Charlotte."

He went inside. He was right about one thing; she never expected to hear his private confessions at their celebration. A twinge of guilt tugged at her chest. Had she stirred this up? Did she push him too far without meaning to?

But there was one part he'd said she wouldn't let go: He had the chance at a family and let it slip away. Did he mean her mom? Was her mom the one that got away?

Chapter 15

Oh No!

Charlotte groaned at the sunlight and buried her face beneath a fluffy pillow. In the dark, she replayed the previous night. It had been after one o'clock by the time she hauled her inebriated aunt into a taxi, and they returned home. Eventually, she worked up the nerve to shove the pillow aside and squinted against the blinding sun, still in last night's outfit.

Sliding out of bed, she shuffled into the living room while throwing her hair up into a messy bun. Peeking over the couch, Aunt Becky was sprawled out on the cushions with one shoe on and one shoe off. "Right where I left you."

Charlotte collected the trail of shoes, purses, and keys from the floor, then dared to nudge her aunt's shoulder. "Aunt Becky?"

A slight groan came from underneath the pillow.

"Aunt Becky, are you alive?" Charlotte yawned as she nudged a little harder.

Another groan emitted from under the pillow as an arm batted the air.

"Aunt Becky, you got to wake up."

Charlotte gave up and went to the kitchen to find something to eat. Pouring herself some orange juice and taking a sip, she came back into the living room and leaned over the couch. She shouted, "Aunt Becky!"

Her aunt shot up, clutched her head, and froze. "What are you trying to do to me?"

"I'm making you pay the consequences for your actions."

"Wait a minute." She started to look around but stopped with a jolt. "How did we get back here? Why am I on the couch?"

"I believe you drank way too much at the party. I tossed you into a cab, and you took yourself to the couch."

Her aunt methodically moved her feet to the floor. "Where's my other Pappagallo pump?"

"I put it in your room."

Aunt Becky groaned as she attempted to stand. "I haven't drunk that much in I don't know how long." Leaning on the counter, she made a face of disgust at the orange juice offered to her.

"You've got to drink and eat. What's good for a hangover?"

"Coffee."

"Coming up." Charlotte started a pot of coffee. "Shame on you, Aunt Becky." She scolded as her aunt pathetically sagged over the kitchen island, cradling her head with both hands. "Hopefully, it was worth it. You seemed to be having a good time."

"I hope I didn't make a fool of myself around all those celebrities. Oh, no," a pitiful groan came from her mouth.

"I think some of them were making fools of themselves right along with you," Charlotte stated. "By the time I got to you, a lot of them were pretty drunk."

"I'm usually so poised. Professional with an easygoing personality." Aunt Becky stared at the patterns on the countertop. "Did you enjoy yourself?"

Charlotte paused before nodding. "Yeah, it was fine. I think you had a better time than me though, it being your type of people."

Her aunt perked up when Charlotte poured her a cup of coffee. She sipped the hot liquid. "Did the night not turn out to be fun for you?"

"I talked with Roy for a bit and Jesse."

The corner of Aunt Becky's mouth twitched upward. "Jesse seems very fond of you. He had nothing but complimentary things to say about you before their show at the Bowl."

"They've all been so nice. I never dreamed they'd invite me to things after the interviews were over."

The thought made Charlotte's heart sink. Until now, she hadn't fully let herself consider what came next. The interviews finished a while ago. She'd been riding high on the invites and rehearsal sit-ins. They even invited her and Aunt Becky backstage after their Thursday show at the Hollywood Bowl, and then that would be it. After that, she wouldn't see them again. Telling Jesse that he was her father was no longer a distant idea, it was imminent. An icy shiver ran through her.

"We should check in with your mom today and tell her all the amazing things we've been doing. Oh, she will be so jealous."

Panic shot throughout her entire body. "About that, do you think we could keep this between us? Not mention it to mom?"

"But bragging to your mom is what I live for."

"Please?"

Aunt Becky straightened up as an eyebrow raised. "How come you don't want to say anything to your mom? Is everything okay between you two?"

"Yes, but remember when you said my grandparents back in the day were so strict with mom when you guys were young? That's kinda how she is with me. She wouldn't be too happy hearing I was at a party with alcohol and such."

"You didn't drink any, did you?"

"No."

"Good." She grabbed her head. "I guess telling Lori wouldn't put me in the greatest of lights."

"And could we keep our meeting with the band a secret too? And the opera?"

"Oh, come on," she whined.

"You can tell her all about them after I leave. Then she won't make me leave early or anything. We can tell her we saw some shows and stuff."

"I'm not sure I understand fully, but my head is pounding. And you're getting good at telling little white lies." She put a hand on her hip. "I don't know if I should be worried or proud."

"I'm a teenager," she said, giving her aunt a gentle hug. "We're not exactly known for spilling all our secrets." She shepherded her aunt to her bedroom. "I'm going to go call Jason. Are you going to be all right by yourself?"

"I'm going to take a hot shower, down a couple of aspirin, lie in bed, and will this hangover away."

Charlotte flopped onto her bed. While mothering her aunt, Charlotte had seen today's date in her aunt's planner. Back home in Oak Falls, they had just completed their summer festival. It was a festival that attracted tourists to their little town. At this fair, vendors sold their homemade goodies and trinkets, people were entertained in various forms, and a large parade with many floats passed through the main street. Every year they had a talent show with prizes, and Britney's solo usually won, even though Olivia was the better singer. They all knew it had to be rigged. She was filled with a sudden, and unexpected, longing for Oak Falls.

Her stomach ached for home. Hearing about the festival from Jason may help with her homesickness. Grabbing the phone to dial, she was startled when it rang in her hand. "Thompson residence."

"Lotty, you're never going to believe what happened. I tried reaching you last night, but you were out."

Her chest tingled, and she grinned from ear to ear at the sound of his voice. "I was at a party."

"I want to hear all about it, but first, I have to tell you something major. I was at the library—"

"Oh, Jason. I want to hear all about the summer festival."

"It was all right. But listen—"

"Did Mr. Patterson do his magic show?"

"Yes, Miss Kyles and your grandad did their exhibitionist painting routine, good painting this time.

"Kim told me before I left that she was going to do a dance."

"She danced, and Olivia sang."

"What'd she sing?"

"She sang an original and killed it."

"Don't tell me, Britney won again."

"You'll never guess what happened."

Charlotte was starving for Oak Falls information. "What?"

"Olivia won."

She sprang forward. "What?! No way. Are you kidding? That is incredible! That is totally awesome. She deserves it so much. Where was Britney? Was she mad? I bet she was."

"Second runner up. And let's just say she was less than amused."

"What did she do?"

"She took her prize and smiled her fake smile, but her eyes were on fire. If looks could kill."

"I can't believe this," Charlotte said as she fell back on the bed. "I am so happy Britney didn't win. I mean . . . I am totally happy for Olivia. She deserved the prize like three years ago."

"Yeah. This summer hasn't been looking too good for Britney. Humiliated by you standing up to her, jealous of your summer, and having to participate in this sham of a show—her words. But that's not why I'm calling—"

"I'm going to have to call Olivia and congratulate her."

Jason exhaled into the phone. "Charlotte—"

"Jason, I have so much to tell you. I was afraid to put any of it on the postcards. But Aunt Becky has all these pictures of her and my mom when they were young. It's totally incredible. There are pictures of my mom kissing Jesse."

"Speaking of Jesse."

"Oh, Jason, he's so incredible. We went to a party for them last night. That's why you couldn't get ahold of me."

"Was there alcohol? Drugs? Did you do any?"

"Jason," she gasped. "I did not. Oof, can you imagine my mom finding out if I had? I wouldn't be able to see Aunt Becky ever again. Speaking of my aunt, she's uh . . . indisposed. Wait a minute."

Charlotte glanced at her door before sitting in the spacious closet. A few dresses hung next to her head.

"Charlotte, I did some digging at the library."

"Why are you still going to the library? Don't you want to hear about all the things I've done with my father? I think . . . I think he wants a family. We've grown closer, and I think he senses what I've been feeling. We're each missing something. I'm a bit nervous, but I can't believe I'm going to tell him I'm his daughter."

"Charlotte. Stop. Talking."

"What's wrong?"

"I've been trying to tell you something."

Charlotte leaned her elbow on her knees. "What's going on?"

"I wouldn't tell him yet about you being his daughter."

"Why? What do you mean? Why wouldn't you want me to tell him?"

Silence.

"Jason, what are you not telling me?"

"I did some more research at the library, poking around and such. And I found something."

"What did you find?" she asked.

"Another connection."

"What are you talking about? What did you find?"

"I found another Jesse Holt."

"Jason?"

"This rock musician, he may not be your dad."

Chapter 16

Betrayal

Charlotte sat up straight and got a face full of a dress hanging in the closet. Brushing it aside, she said, "What do you mean, this Jesse Holt isn't my father?"

"I'm just saying, he may not be."

"You better start making sense." Her heart raced a million miles a minute.

Jason cleared his throat; the rustle of papers came through the line. "Um, okay. So I found him in the obituary. Back in 1978 a college student by the name of Jesse Holt from one of our neighboring towns was struck by a car and killed. He was about twenty-one. Studying accounting." He paused. "He and your mom ran in the same circles."

Charlotte shook her head.

"I pulled out old news articles about the crash. It even made the paper here in Oak Falls. I tracked down his high school yearbook. There's pictures of him, Lotty. He . . . he kind of looks like you."

"No. I don't believe this," she said automatically.

"There's more."

"But the pictures." Charlotte's voice cracked. "You didn't see the pictures out here."

Jason continued gently, "In the junior prom section, there's a photo of your mom. She's standing with a group of people by a punch bowl. Jesse Holt is beside her. Her name is printed underneath." He hesitated. "And there's another photo of a group of juniors and seniors. Your mom is laughing as he's kissing her cheek."

Her heart pounded in her ears.

"Your mom knew him," Jason said. "It's a strong connection."

"No." Her chest tightened. "No. It's not true."

"Lotty. I'm sorry. But now that there's two connections, you may need to rethink things. Maybe your mom never talked about your father because he died."

It was hard to breathe. "I . . . I gotta go."

"Lotty. Lotty, wait."

She hung up the phone. Frozen in the closet. This couldn't be possible. How was this possible?

Her mind spun.

Her heart ached.

Her stomach churned.

She'd been so happy, filled with something warm and new. She had let herself believe, let herself hope and dream. But now that happiness turned to grief, grief for a man she never knew. Could this quiet, ordinary boy be her father? An accounting student who died before she got a chance to know him.

Charlotte threw her head back and let out a small sob. Everything had finally made sense. She was so close to answers, and now all she had were more questions.

This wasn't fair.

Old memories gushed to the surface. She was seven again, ear pressed against the crack in the door, straining to listen to her grandma and mother.

"She's incomplete . . ."

Those words stung. She had trusted her grandmother but instead felt ripped open by her callous comments. They affected her more than her grandma would ever know.

Another memory surfaced. Lying on a picnic blanket with her grandpa, watching the clouds. His words stuck out like a sore thumb.

"Stories about where you come from are a special thing. They help you understand yourself a little better . . ."

She was trying, and now it felt like she was being punished.

And what gave Britney the right to talk about her the way she did? "Your mom's a slut, and you're a bastard . . ."

The worst part, Charlotte hated to admit, was that Britney might be right.

She wiped away the tears and buried her head in her arms, propped against her knees. Britney was right. More tears dropped into her lap.

For so long she'd been stuck, unable to move forward. This summer had been a chance for answers, possibilities, and filling that gaping hole inside her. She'd found him and started to love him. But now what?

The phone rang. She groaned. She didn't want to answer it, but her aunt was sleeping in the next room.

"Hello?"

"Hi, Charlotte."

Charlotte rolled her eyes at the sound of her mom's voice. "Hey."

"Is something wrong?"

"No."

"Did something happen? You don't sound yourself."

Charlotte sighed. "I'm fine."

"Are you sure?"

"Yes, Mom." She couldn't hide her irritation.

Silence hung between them before Lori continued, "Well, what have you both been up to lately?"

Charlotte pulled her brows together and chewed on a strand of hair. Everything bubbled at the surface, threatening to explode. "Not much."

Silence.

"Oh. Why won't you talk to me?" Her mom sounded a little disappointed.

"Why have you been calling so much?"

"Because I miss you. Charlotte, are you sure nothing happened?"

"You've been taking more of an interest in what I've been doing this summer than you have in years. You keep calling asking what we've done. You don't ask about me. You ask about what we've done. It's almost like you're jealous. Jealous that you're not out here reliving your younger days."

"Charlotte," her mom breathed her name in surprise.

"I've seen the pictures of you partying and being reckless. Now it's like you're someone totally different. You're some boring person who cares too much about what others think rather than just being who you used to be, fun and carefree. Aunt Becky is still wild and free and easy. She doesn't care what other people think of her."

"Charlotte—"

"Just stop calling. Stop trying to pry information out of me so you can feel something." She slammed the phone down, then took it off the receiver so her mom couldn't call back.

Charlotte leaned her head back on the wall. Her veins pumped furiously. She had never talked to her mom like that before, and she would pay for it later. But right now, she didn't care. It had to be said.

Charlotte groaned and fell dramatically onto the floor, half her body spilling out of the closet. She stared at the ceiling, replaying her conversation with Jason. Was Jason right? Could this accounting student have been her father? There was a connection. They'd known each other. But how well? Was it just platonic or more?

Well, one thing was for sure, he fit her mom's persona to a tea. Boring. Business oriented. She was in real estate. He wanted to be an accountant. Did they fall in love in college? Was his tragic death too painful to talk about?

Life sucked.

For the last month, she had let herself imagine being the musician's daughter.

But now, she had to reframe herself with this other man. Accounting was a respectable job. Ordinary, if she was being honest. She pictured him in his nine-to-five job, pulling into the driveway, playing with her in the yard, shoveling snow, and building snowmen.

Summer evenings would've been spent on the front porch with

her parents, watching the sunset. They'd have neighborhood walks. He might've taught her to ride a bike. Maybe she would've had a brother or sister. Picturesque. But it never happened. His life had been cut short.

Charlotte grabbed her head. What she wouldn't give to have the musician as her father. Dropping her arms to the carpet, she let out one more dramatic exhale but stopped short.

Wait a minute.

She shot up on her elbows.

Among this new information, one thing didn't fit. She even blurted it out to her mom. This new Jesse Holt matched her mom's current, businesslike persona, not who she had been when she was young. Her mom had been wild and full of life. The musician better fit that past, the one Charlotte had only glimpsed through photos and stories. Being in California had shown her just how different her mom used to be.

Charlotte leapt to her feet. The would-be accountant may be a good candidate, but that's all he was—a candidate.

By contrast, the musician was someone her mom knew, someone alive, and someone whose path intertwined with her mom's life. Charlotte had photographic proof, and Aunt Becky was an eyewitness.

Pacing now, hope filled her again. The musician. He was it. He was her father. He had to be.

Charlotte dove for the phone in the closet and dialed Jason's number. On the second ring, he answered.

"Hunter residence."

"Jason, this new Jesse can't be my father. He can't be. It doesn't fit."

"Lotty, what are you saying?"

"Mom wasn't the type to date an accountant back then. The musician was more her type."

"That might be, but it's too far-fetched. Isn't it more plausible that your mom is sad about your birth father's death? And that's why she can't talk about it? It makes more sense than a one-night stand with a musician."

"Maybe in your photos, she was someone's date at a different school. But you haven't seen the pictures I have out here. I'm talking several years of connection. Then there's all the evidence. Jesse, the musician, even said he let someone slip away years ago. That's my mom. It's him."

Silence again.

Jason spoke carefully, "I'm starting to think this wasn't a good idea."

"What do you mean?"

"I don't think you should tell this musician he's your father."

"How can you say that?"

"Lotty, I think you're getting too caught up in this. I don't want to see you get hurt."

Charlotte's eyes burned. "What are you saying? You helped me. You wanted to help me find him. To find my father."

"I did. But I think we need to stop now. It's not some dream anymore. We're talking about real people and real lives." He hesitated. "I don't know. This Jesse who died in college made me realize—this is real. We're dealing with real people."

"I'm also real, Jase. With real feelings."

"I know. I want you to be happy. But it isn't just about you. If you tell the musician, it's about him too. It'd disrupt his life."

"Disrupt? Am I a burden now?"

"No. That's not what I meant."

"He wants a family. He wants this."

"Or so you think."

"Why are you saying this?" Charlotte's heart shattered into little pieces. He was abandoning the project they had started together.

"Charlotte, I think it's time you came home. I miss you. We all miss you. I'll help you figure out what you want to be when you grow up. Just come home."

"It's not just that. This entire search is about who I am as a person."

"I don't think you can find the answers you want in your father."

"You don't want me to have a family," she said through gritted teeth. Even as she said it, she knew it wasn't true. But the hurt and anger in her chest needed someone to blame, and Jason was an easy target.

"Yes, I do. You're not listening,"

"Oh, I'm listening very well. Now you listen, Jason. You may have the perfect family, but don't try and stop me from finding mine."

"Charlotte—"

"Tomorrow, I'm going to tell him that he's my father at the Hollywood Bowl. And I'm going to tell him whether you like it or not." And before he could protest further, she cut him off by hanging up the phone.

She let the phone slip from her hand and onto the bed. How could Jason do this to her? He was her closest friend, the one who helped her, and now it felt like a betrayal.

Still in last night's clothes, she didn't care. The weight in her chest pulled her down. She collapsed onto her bed, crying softly into a pillow until her throat ached and her eyes burned. It felt like she had been stabbed and gutted. When the tears finally ran dry, she dragged herself into the living room.

Aunt Becky was still passed out, the radio playing quietly in her room. To keep herself from sobbing again, Charlotte turned on the TV and stared blankly at *The Fresh Prince of Bel-Air*.

Jason's betrayal and the fight with her mom—this had to be the worst day of her life.

Will Smith's character peeked around a corner while Carlton danced. Normally, she would've laughed. Not today. Her vision grew fuzzy. The TV wasn't helping. She needed to do something to keep from spiraling.

She barely registered the quiet movement in the room before her aunt appeared and settled beside her, pressing a cold compress to her forehead. Together they spent the rest of the afternoon half watching several movies. It filled the time but not her thoughts. Her mind kept wandering back to the phone conversations with Jason and her mom. She shook her head and gritted her teeth, willing herself not to cry. Jason was wrong, and she was about to prove it.

Chapter 17

I'm Your Daughter

Charlotte sat in front of the vanity, staring at her reflection.

Dipping her brush in her blush compact, she tapped it, then gently brushed it on her cheek. Everything must be absolutely perfect. It was a big night. Tonight, she was going to tell Jesse Holt she was his daughter. Aunt Becky's boss came through and got them seats near the front of the stage.

She glanced at the clock.

Five hours, twenty minutes, and thirty seconds until the Hollywood Bowl.

Her back stiffened a little as Jason's hurtful words replayed in her mind. "Don't cry," she scolded the pesky tears threatening to surface.

What she was doing was right. It had to be. Once and for all, she'd prove to Jason, her mom, and herself that finding her father was the key to finding herself. Only then would life finally make sense.

Charlotte swiped an applicator in a warm taupe eyeshadow powder. Several CoverGirl eye shadow palettes lay open on the vanity, ranging from lavender plum, olive green, to chocolate brown, all colors to enhance her hazel eyes. She blended it into her crease and daydreamed about life with her father.

As a musician, he traveled a lot. He'd be gone for several months, but when he came home, they'd make the most of it. They'd talk for hours and hours on the front porch, take long drives in his classic convertible, and dream about the future over boysenberry pie.

She smiled.

Her future.

Something she never thought about.

Charlotte combed her hair and stood looking at the outfits displayed on her bed. Four options and it was difficult.

Aunt Becky glided into the bedroom with a glass of tea. "For you."

"Thank you." Charlotte smiled as the delicious amber liquid cooled her throat.

Both of them stared at the outfits on the bed. "Struggling with a decision?"

Charlotte nodded.

"I understand." Aunt Becky stepped closer and studied each and every outfit.

Charlotte readily accepted her aunt's fashion advice. Her aunt was the best-dressed person she knew, elegant even in her nightgowns.

"I'd go with this one. It's spunky but gives you a sense of class and elegance, without looking slutty." Aunt Becky laughed.

Charlotte studied the chosen outfit. It was a good one. A patterned top with tapered straps and a black miniskirt, black tights, and her black Doc Marten boots. She had a little black purse to pair with it. Nodding in approval, she said, "Sounds good."

Aunt Becky grabbed Charlotte's hand. "Now, come help me pick out my own outfit."

Forty minutes and twenty-five seconds.

They walked out of the apartment. Charlotte wore her outfit with a swipe of burgundy lipstick on her lips. Aunt Becky could be a model in her red sleeveless turtleneck tucked into black slacks with a belt and fancy buckle, black flats, and tousled golden hair.

Charlotte hadn't eaten anything. She was too nervous. The

butterflies in her stomach were in full flight, and her palms were sweaty.

On the walk to the amphitheater, she pretended to listen to Aunt Becky's idle chatter. Her aunt was never at a loss for conversation, which helped curb Charlotte's unending nerves. As they neared the sidewalks clustered with people in a line, they filed behind. The energy level in the crowd was high. Charlotte still couldn't believe it. Caravan had the power to invoke such electric energy.

Charlotte grabbed her aunt's wristwatch. Thirty minutes until the show. During The Three Tenors, Jesse had invited them backstage after. She decided that's when she'd finally pull him aside and tell him. No more rush before the show.

After showing their tickets, they descended unending stairs to the front row of the garden section.

Charlotte checked her aunt's watch.

Fifteen minutes.

Charlotte scanned the crowd. The sold-out amphitheater filled fast. As murmurs surged through the crowd, she smiled, remembering her father beside her just days ago at the opera. But this was far more exciting.

Charlotte checked her aunt's watch again.

Eight minutes.

"Why do you keep looking at the time? Are you expecting something?"

Charlotte gave a nervous smile. "Oh, no. I'm excited for the show to start."

"Does it feel weird not meeting them before like you usually do?" Aunt Becky asked.

"Yes."

"You've met them?" A guy beside her interjected, a Joey Lawrence wannabe with large round glasses.

Charlotte nodded.

Aunt Becky proudly furthered, "She's writing an article. They kindly let her interview them."

His mouth gaped open. "No way. That's totally awesome. What are they like?"

"They are real nice guys. Pretty funny."

"And your article. What's it for? Some newspaper or something?"

"It's for my school paper." This was the last time she'd use this excuse.

Disbelief creased his face. "And they let you talk to them because of that?"

Straightening her back and lifting her nose, she turned toward the stage. She didn't need to defend herself.

As Aunt Becky made small talk with someone next to her, Charlotte sat quietly, ignoring the *Blossom* look-alike whispering to his friends about her.

The sun started to dip in the sky.

Her legs bounced restlessly.

Aunt Becky's watch read one minute.

The sun slipped behind the mountains as the stage lights flared, then cut to black. The crowd cheered, then fell suddenly silent.

The drumsticks counted off, then erupted into rapid runs down the toms. The audience burst into cheers as the "Tears from the Gallows" riff began. Everyone shot to their feet. White lights cut across the stage. Reggie's bass boomed, and Jesse's guitar shredded. The song climbed, and the crowd went nuts when Danny took the stage.

Song after song, the crowd sang in euphoric unison. The night raced by on sheer energy. About halfway through the show, Danny paced the stage while speaking into the microphone. "We want to do something a little bit different tonight. We wrote a song recently. And we think it's one heckuva song. And if it's all right with you, we're going to play it for you tonight!"

The crowd roared with deafening cheers. Caravan leaned into their microphones and sang an intricate and powerful a cappella harmony.

Charlotte seized her aunt's arm. "This is the song! The one I told you about. They're doing it."

Roy played a series of fills on the toms into the first verse. Danny held a beautiful note at the bridge, launching Jesse's guitar solo. He stepped to the edge of the stage, caught Charlotte in the crowd and smiled.

Tears poured out before she realized it, and she laughed through them. She loved him with her whole heart. For the first time, she let herself feel what it meant to have a father.

The music stopped abruptly, and their harmonies carried the final notes alone.

The amphitheater shook with the audience's uproar.

The band bowed as Danny went to the front of the stage. "Thank you! That's called 'Shadows Rising.' Glad you agree with us." He laughed. "We wanted to dedicate this song to our friend Charlotte Reynolds." Danny shaded his eyes to scan the crowd. "She's here somewhere."

Heart pounding, Charlotte sank into her chair, but her aunt snatched her arm, pulled her to her feet to wave her arm.

Danny pointed her way with a big sparkling smile. "There she is. That was for you."

Charlotte offered a sheepish smile as all eyes turned toward her, and she mouthed thank you. Relief washed over her as Danny spoke, taking the attention off her.

Charlotte caught Jesse looking at her. He laughed, reading her embarrassment. Hitching her hands on her hips, she shook her head and scrunched her nose at him.

Their moment ended as Danny walked over to talk to him.

"Whoa, you do know them," the doubting Joey Lawrence exclaimed. "I thought you were making it up."

Charlotte gave a terse expression, returning her attention to the concert. While the rest of the show was phenomenal, her stomach churned and her heart beat wildly with each passing song. The concert was coming to a close. It became difficult to enjoy the show. Soon hearing it became a chore over her thunderous heartbeat. Her throat and lips were dry.

Then came the inevitable: the final song, followed by a bow, and an encore. During the last bow, Roy made eye contact with her, tossing her his drumstick.

Charlotte decided to be nice and offered the guy sitting next to her the drumstick. He thanked her a bunch before leaving with his friends.

The audience started to filter up the aisles.

It was time.

Charlotte hesitated as Aunt Becky stepped into the aisle. "Let's go. Don't want to keep them waiting," she said in her cheery voice.

She followed, though her feet felt slower this time. Her stomach fluttered as they moved into the narrow service alley running alongside the stage, the same one cordoned off with ropes and security guards. A tall guard displayed his hands as they approached.

"We have backstage passes," Aunt Becky said as she produced their tickets. The guard scanned them and stepped aside.

The alley opened onto a small side wing of the stage. Caravan's canvas tent loomed ahead, tucked behind stacked equipment and lighting cases. Crew members wove in and out, coiling cables and hauling gear.

Aunt Becky approached the tent, but Charlotte froze, her mouth dry as cotton and her stomach queasy.

"Um . . . give me a moment."

"Is something wrong?"

"No. You go on ahead. I need just a second." Charlotte's knees knocked together.

"I'm not leaving you out here by yourself."

Charlotte rolled her eyes with a forced grin. "You know you want to see Danny. I'll be right in. Just give me a second."

Aunt Becky was pushed toward the pop-up tent.

Charlotte leaned against a parked van, taking a few deep breaths to calm her stomach. This was it. The moment she had been dreaming of for so long.

It was so close.

Frighteningly close.

Dreaming was safe.

Reality was dangerous.

Echoes and murmurs of the lingering crowd drifted through the air, fading into the night. Before too long, a flap of the tent opened, and Jesse Holt stepped out with a cigarette in his hand. He spotted her a few paces away against the van. "I was told there was a young lady refusing to come see us."

Why did he have to come out now?

Charlotte gulped down the queasiness. "I needed some air. Funny isn't it, with the concert being outside and all."

"Are you getting sick?"

"No. I'm all right." This was happening. "Aren't you afraid of getting attacked by adoring fans?"

He waved the notion away with his cigarette hand. "I'll risk it. You should come see your teacher. She is making Danny sign a bunch of stuff." He chuckled.

Don't chicken out. It's time.

"I can't believe this is the last time we'll be seeing you. Well, I hope not. You've become a fixture among us. Roy's your biggest fan."

Charlotte grinned. She liked Roy a lot. "It'd be real nice to see you all again." Her hands were in sweaty knots. "I have a confession to make. Yes, another one." She giggled nervously. "I hope you won't think less of me. All right, here it goes. She's not really my teacher. She's my aunt. My godmother, actually. I'm not explaining myself very well. She and my mom are best friends and . . . I don't know why I lied. And I can't believe she went along with the lie, but that's kind of her personality, being a spontaneous person. Not a habitual liar."

He raised a brow but had a smile on his face. At least he didn't appear too upset.

"I'm sorry I lied."

He shrugged. "I don't care."

Charlotte blew out some air. "Speaking of Aunt Becky and my mom, there's been something I've been wanting to tell you." Her mouth was so dry.

A few stagehands passed by and congratulated the guitarist on the show.

A ball formed in her throat and her jaw trembled. "Look, I'm going to preface this by saying this is going to sound totally insane and unbelievable, and you're going to think I've gone off my rocker."

"Okay." He chuckled and took a puff from his cigarette.

"Writing this article wasn't the only reason I'm here hanging out with you guys. In fact, the article was kind of a ruse."

His face changed, and she winced.

"I'm just going to say it." She took a breath and dared to look at him. "I think I may be your daughter."

He froze.

For a long, terrible eternity.

He cleared his throat, eyes darting to the side as he shifted his weight.

And before she knew it, everything Charlotte had been holding onto—all the evidence, the pictures, the whole story—tumbled out. For the first time in months, she was empty of secrets. Drawing a deep breath, she wiped the tears that formed.

"I've never known my father, and I had to find out for myself who he was. I just wanted to find my dad."

His eyes never left the ground, furthering the distance between the two of them. Clearing his throat, he stamped out his cigarette and stuffed his hands into his pockets.

Charlotte tried to calm the terror radiating from him. "I know it's a lot." Did he even believe her? Was this a mistake? Maybe this wasn't a good idea. "I'm sorry. I'm realizing now that I probably shouldn't have told you."

"Charlotte?"

Charlotte stilled, stunned by the familiar voice calling her name. She slowly turned.

"Mom?"

Chapter 18

Lori

Her mom rushed down the service drive, dodged a stagehand, and flung her arms around her daughter while Matt trailed behind.

Charlotte ripped away from her mother's embrace. "Mom, what are you doing here?"

"Jason called. I was so worried about you."

"Jason?" She couldn't believe it. "How could he do that?"

"He was also worried about you." Lori recognized the musician standing quietly to the side.

For the first time in years her mom and dad were together. It was now or never. "Actually, this couldn't be better timing." A glimmer of hope ignited in her as she turned toward her father.

"She can explain everything—how you two had me and why she refused to tell me about you. I still don't understand why she kept me from you, but it doesn't matter now. We can finally be a family."

"Charlotte, this isn't the time—" Lori started.

"Yes, it is. Don't you see—?"

Jesse scratched the back of his head. "Charlotte, I don't know what to say—"

"It's all right. I know this is really awkward. But soon it'll be something we can laugh at."

"Charlotte, honey."

"Tell him, Mom. Explain everything and I'll be—"

"Honey, stop." Lori's voice cracked as she grabbed her daughter's shoulders. "Charlotte, I think we've taken up enough of Mr. Holt's time."

Jesse gave a tense, cordial grin and took a step back.

Charlotte's brow lowered. "Mr. Holt? Mom, why so formal? No, tell him I'm his daughter. You two met back in the '70s. I saw all the pictures."

Jesse and Lori exchanged a confused glance between each other.

Charlotte tugged on her mom's arm. "You two remember, don't you?"

The tent flap opened, and Aunt Becky stepped out. "What's taking you so long, girl—" Seeing her best friend made her stop short. "Lori? What on earth are you doing here? It didn't take you long to reunite with your childhood crush." Her eyes sparkled at the guitarist.

Charlotte snatched her aunt's arm. "Aunt Becky, tell them. Tell them about all the pictures. The picture of them kissing. About the parties you all went to. How they knew each other and how mom got pregnant from him. It's all right. I'm old enough to know."

Aunt Becky's expression widened, her breath catching. "Is that why you did this? Oh, no. Oh, Charlotte." She turned to Lori. "I swear I had no idea that's why she came out here."

The canvas tent flap rustled open again. One by one, the band members drifted out, curiosity written across their faces.

Lori noticed them too. Tears fell as she cupped her daughter's cheeks. "Honey, let's go talk about this in private."

"Tell me he's my father." Charlotte pointed, her hand shaking, straight at the guitarist.

Lori followed the gesture. She looked at Jesse for a long, aching moment before turning back to her daughter. Her voice was soft as she spoke, "No, honey. Jesse Holt is not your father."

Something inside Charlotte fractured. Her limbs shook as hot tears burned her eyes. She shook her head. "No. No. No. But my birth certificate. We look alike . . . we . . . the time fits."

Lori swallowed and brushed her daughter's hair aside. "Charlotte, your father was someone I knew for only a few years. He was wild and made bad choices." Her voice cracked as she continued, "He passed away before you were born."

Charlotte stumbled back, shaking her head in denial.

"I was so ashamed. Ashamed of being suckered into his charms. He wasn't always a nice man. I'm so sorry. Honey, I'm so sorry."

"No, no."

Everything spun. She reached blindly for the side of the van—and that's when she saw them. All of them.

Outside the tent, the band stood in silence. They'd heard every word. Charlotte's skin burned with humiliation that outweighed her grief.

"I never wanted you to know because it wasn't a pretty picture." Her throat choked a sob. "I thought keeping it from you was kinder."

"But . . . the pictures," Charlotte whispered, clinging to a sliver of hope.

"I was a fan who had backstage passes. I snuck backstage and went to after-parties. That's all," Lori answered.

For her last attempt, she said, "But my birth certificate."

"It says Jesse Hait," Lori said gently.

She gasped as that night rushed back, reading her birth certificate in the glow of the moonlight, and seeing it only for a split second. Did she really misread something so important? What had she done? Her whole body trembled. She covered her mouth to stop the threatening nausea.

"Charlotte?" Jesse took a step forward.

A sob broke from her lips, and she choked in embarrassment. She couldn't look at him. Couldn't look at any of them. She had to get away.

"I can't believe this is happening." She pushed past them all, running up the service drive, nearly colliding with Matt.

He trailed after her.

"Charlotte," Lori called after her.

"Hey, I'm sorry," Jesse said as he stopped her. "I'm sorry I wasn't her father." There was no anger or annoyance, only sincerity in his eyes.

"Thank you," Lori said, then ran after her daughter.

Becky exchanged glances with Jesse before loosely throwing up her hands and following them.

Matt stood by his car door as Charlotte vomited into a bush. "You okay?"

Charlotte stood and wiped her mouth. "Take me back to the apartment."

"Should we wait for your mom?"

"That's the last thing I want." She slid into the passenger seat.

He hesitated before getting in and putting the keys in the ignition. They filed out of the parking lot and onto the road.

"What are you doing here anyway? And with my mom?"

He sighed before explaining how he got the CliffsNotes version from his frantic cousin who begged him to pick up her mother from the airport to stop Charlotte from confronting the musician. "I knew you were up to something," he said lightly, but her cold silence killed any further conversation. When he put the car in park, he said, "I think what you did . . . well, you've got guts for believing in something so much to fly across an entire country to get it."

By the time Lori and her aunt reached the apartment, Charlotte had made up her mind. She was going home. Tonight.

Charlotte stood resolutely like a statue in the kitchen as her mom paced the living room with the phone pressed to her ear. Aunt Becky sat on the couch glancing between mother and daughter. The cheery music crackling through the phone while her mom was on hold contrasted with the tension in the apartment.

A feminine voice replaced the music. Lori sat on the coffee table as she listened to the list of available flights. She gave her credit card number, finalized boarding information, then hung up the phone.

A red-eye flight at two in the morning. Two seats but not together.

Charlotte locked herself in her room after that and didn't come out until it was time to leave.

Aunt Becky ordered a taxi, and they rode to the airport in silence. No one knew what to say. The long drive was unbearable.

At the curb, Becky hugged Charlotte tightly, then leaned in to whisper something to Lori. Her mom nodded.

They boarded the plane without another word. Charlotte didn't remember falling asleep. The next thing she knew, the cabin lights turned on, and the pilot announced their arrival.

Dazed.

Unfeeling.

Hollow.

Once inside her Oak Falls bedroom, she finally broke down, collapsing into a puddle on her bed and muffling her cries into her pillow.

She was never leaving her room again. The shame. The embarrassment. The guilt. Words couldn't capture it. It was all for nothing. It was all her fault, all because she misread her birth certificate. How stupid could she be to misread something so important?

What must he think of her? She'd wasted every minute of the musician's time. And the absolute worst, most depressing thing of all was now she knew the truth. Her real father was dead.

Back in Aunt Becky's apartment, her mom confessed to her father being a hippie and a drug addict who'd accidentally overdosed. Now she'd never have a chance to get to know him, meaning that the empty part of her would never be filled.

She felt utterly worthless.

The product of booze and drugs.

A bastard child.

Charlotte pulled a fluffy purple pillow to her chest and buried her face. Those girls at the potluck were right. She was a mistake. She was nothing. She believed once she discovered her father she'd feel something. But there was nothing there. She was numb.

Time lost all meaning in the dark. She didn't know if she'd slept or not, only that she woke up on the floor, arms outstretched. Her fingertips brushed something underneath the bed that caught her attention.

Tears welled again as she pulled out the stack of Caravan's records. There on top sat her sketch pad with Jesse Holt's face staring back at her.

A gentle knock sounded on her door. "Charlotte? Can we talk?"

Ignoring her mother, she crawled back into bed, burying herself in her pillows.

Time passed. Charlotte sat on her floor, staring mindlessly at her stereo. The front door screeched on its hinges as footsteps clunked up the porch steps. Hushed voices carried faintly through the screen door.

" . . . She's still not talking to me. Only comes out for barely any food and water."

Charlotte froze. It wasn't her grandparents, was it? They had tried talking to her the day before. She wasn't opening the door for them, especially her grandmother.

A soft laugh floated down the hall. A familiar laugh.

Aunt Becky. She was on the front porch.

Charlotte's stomach twisted. Why did she have to come? It felt like she'd brought all that shame and pain from California straight into Oak Falls, into her bedroom, forcing it all to the surface again. Charlotte wanted to crawl back into bed. But she stayed at the door, straining to hear.

She turned the handle and cracked the door. Their voices were low, and Charlotte opened it a little wider, stepping into the hall.

"It's so unbelievable what she did. I should've known something was up when she wanted me to keep secrets from you, laying it out all innocent like."

"We used to do that."

Charlotte's brow furrowed. Were they talking about her?

"I should've noticed the warning signs. I'm just not a seasoned mother such as yourself."

"I'm her mother, and I missed all the signs myself. Telling me she wanted to hang out with you so suddenly. I should've sensed something was up. It wasn't until she blew up at me on the phone when I realized something was truly wrong."

"She did that?" Aunt Becky asked in disbelief.

"And I tried to call back but couldn't get through."

"That little fool unplugged my phone. I had noticed it unplugged right before the concert. Thought it was an accident."

"That explains why I couldn't reach you."

Tiptoeing carefully over the squeaky part of the hall floor, Charlotte crept into the dark living room. Through the sheer curtains of the front window, she saw her mom and Aunt Becky on the patio and listened silently.

"Lori, I had no idea. I hope you know that. I would never have encouraged this to go to the level it did."

"I know."

Becky sat back in her chair, rocking gently. "And all I did was feed her suspicions with stories of us meeting them and showing her all of those pictures of us back in the day."

A sharp pain tightened in Charlotte's chest. Those pictures burned in her memory, pictures that showed what might've been. She hugged her arms, inching toward the couch under the window.

Lori's voice was shaky. "Charlotte told me I was jealous of her time out there with you. It made me angry. I was ready to give her a few choice words over the phone. But . . ."

Charlotte pressed closer to the window, almost holding her breath.

"But I think she was right. That's why I got so angry."

Her stomach flipped. She'd been right about something?

Lori continued, "Her being out there this whole time made me realize how much I'd been taking her for granted here. I missed her so much. I didn't like coming home to an empty and quiet house."

Tears welled up in Charlotte's eyes. She quietly wiped them away.

"And what hurt so much was realizing how much of my true self I've stopped being. Hearing everything you guys did made me miss what we did. After I had Charlotte, I tried for so long to prove to the people here that I wasn't the slut they thought I was. Believe me, I saw the looks and heard the whispers. I'm sure some still think that of me. Even my own parents remind me from time to time. I had to bury that fun part of myself and show them someone different."

"Why?" Becky asked.

Charlotte mouthed the word, silently echoing Becky's same question.

"So I could make something of myself."

Charlotte clung to a pillow, aching for the fun-loving mom she hadn't seen in years.

"I'm still surprised they let you come out to see me every summer. By the way, how are your *lovely* parents?" Aunt Becky's sarcasm was unmistakable.

Lori chuckled mildly. "My mother and I still butt heads from time to time. But they love Charlotte. And I needed them to help me with her, especially when she was younger."

"I'm sure they used their Southern charm to politely pressure you into marrying someone."

"All the time. But I couldn't think of marrying after what I went through. I shut that part of myself away." Lori leaned forward on her legs. "I thought ignoring my past indiscretions was the answer. As if thinking it never happened was the solution. It made things worse." She sniffed. "I thought being successful would make up for everything."

Charlotte's heart plummeted. Was that the reason for her distance?

"I could see that in this town." Becky's voice was gentle.

"I wanted to show all of them. It drove me. And in the process, I wound up pushing my own daughter away. We used to bake. All the time. Her little feet on the step stool, barely reaching the counter as she made an absolute mess scooping the batter into the muffin tin. We used to have the best talks."

Another tear fell onto the pillow. Charlotte cherished those memories, longing for them still.

"What happened?"

Lori sighed. "Oh, I don't know. I think it was a lot of little things, but one that comes to mind was at my great-aunt's funeral. My mother and I argued. My past came up as it usually did. But this time she said some things that—I don't know—put me in overdrive. I dove headfirst into my job to prove to her that I wasn't a failure. To prove to myself I wasn't a failure."

Becky took her friend's hand. "But you lost part of yourself. I miss that part of my best friend. I haven't seen her in a long time."

"I know," Lori whispered. "And now I hope it's not too late to fix this."

"It's not too late. But you've got to start being honest with her. Give her the answers she's been looking for." Aunt Becky pulled out a thick photo album that looked like it was bursting at the seams. She handed it to her mom who brushed the cover with her fingers. "Tell her about her father."

Lori's voice dropped to a whisper. "I'm scared. Telling her the truth about her father."

"Are you scared to tell Charlotte about her father or what she'll think of you? Lori, nobody's perfect. Charlotte knows that. Who knows, this may bring you closer than you've ever been."

Lori sniffed and wiped her cheeks.

Charlotte looked up at the porch light, listening to the bugs buzzing around it and the crickets out in the darkness. Her hand hovered near the door handle. She was about to open it when her aunt's playful voice broke the silence. "You'll never guess who came to visit me. I still can't believe Charlotte cooked up this scheme and got into the good graces of one of our most favorite bands."

Lori laughed weakly. "I couldn't believe it when I heard it from Jason. It's almost . . . I'm still at a loss for words. So which one knocked on your door?"

"Jesse Holt from Caravan. He was looking for you."

Lori and Becky laughed. "He still looks so good, I have to admit," Lori said.

"Your daughter has guts. Just like her mother. Remember their after-party? The one we hitchhiked to for their San Francisco concert?"

"Oh, don't remind me." Lori covered her face.

Becky squealed. "The look on Jesse's baby face. I swear his eyes were about to pop out of his head at what you did."

"I had to get his attention somehow."

"And boy you did. I was never that bold. There's layers to you, girl. And for the rest of the night, he talked to you."

"And several other nights. We became quite friendly. He was one of the good ones."

"He's still just as nice. He said he'd grown very fond of Charlotte. She seems to have an effect on the people she meets. I'd say that's a reflection on you. You're not a total failure," she said lightly, and her friend chuckled.

"Charlotte is pretty special," Lori admitted.

"Help her see that," Becky encouraged. "Now, what does a girl have to do to get some wine around here?"

The hinges on the front door screeched and both women turned.

Chapter 19

Who Is Charlotte Reynolds?

Jason took the familiar path to their spot in Meadow Park. Through the trees, he spotted Charlotte sitting on the grass, oblivious even when a twig snapped beneath his shoe.

Flicking back his shaggy hair, he spoke carefully. "Hey, Lotty. I haven't seen you since you've been back."

"I haven't felt like seeing anyone." She sighed.

He bit his lip, then kicked a pebble into the water. "Um . . . Kim's been calling me. Olivia too. They're worried about you. We all are."

"I don't feel like talking to anyone either."

"This isn't right, you isolating yourself like this."

"Please, Jason."

"I think you might feel better if you let it out."

"Just leave me alone." There was a little bit of oomph behind her voice.

"No. No, I'm not going to do that. I'm not going to let you pull away from everyone over this."

"Why should I talk to you about it when you have no idea what I'm going through?" Charlotte stood and faced him.

"You're right. I don't truly know. But I know what hurt and sadness feel like."

"You couldn't possibly understand. You've always had the perfect family," a mild sneer in her voice.

There was silence between them. Birds sang a happy tune to one another, unaware of the seriousness of their conversation.

"Why do you always have to insult my family?"

Charlotte's eyes scrunched into a question. "What are you talking about?"

"All our lives, you've made jabs or poked fun at me and my family. Whether on purpose or not, it's like you're trying to make me feel guilty for having the family I have. And I've always felt guilty around you." He paused, then continued, "But I'm not going to feel guilty for it anymore. You need to look at your own family and be grateful for who you have."

"Ha, what family? A dead father and a mother I've had a complicated relationship with. One you called, by the way, and told all my secrets to." Charlotte shook her head. "How could you do that?"

"Because I was worried about you."

"You had no right to call her."

"What would you have done if your mom didn't come to rescue you? Had you thought about that?"

Charlotte exhaled and fought back the eruption of tears threatening to surface.

"Charlotte, what is going on? I know you had your heart set on Holt being your dad, but now you have the answers. That's all you've wanted. Talk to me. Yell at me. Something."

She stared blankly at the opposite end of the creek. "Everything I did this summer, every decision I made, every feeling I believed in was all for nothing. Absolutely nothing."

"That's not true."

Charlotte turned to him, eyes welling up with tears. They were mixed with anger and fear. "I feel nothing. My life feels just as it did before I even started looking into who my father was. Which means I am nothing."

"Come on, you're not nothing."

"Yes, I am. And I'm going to be stuck forever. Never knowing."

Jason tilted his chin up at the trees before committing to what he was about to say. "I hoped you'd find your father, but I never imagined you'd discover what you were really looking for."

"What did you say?"

"I didn't think finding your father would solve your problem."

"Thanks for believing in me," she shot back. "I thought you were my best friend."

"I am."

"Best friends have each other's backs."

"I do have your back."

"My best friend would believe in me and help me—"

"Best friends also tell the truth, no matter how hard it may hurt." He stepped toward her, letting his arms drop. "Lotty, I already think you're enough just being you. You're already whole."

Charlotte looked away, tears burning her eyes.

"You want to know who Charlotte Reynolds is? She is a warm and kindhearted person." He stepped closer. "Ever since you were a kid, you've helped people. You always thought of others. You've volunteered at the senior citizen center bringing smiles to all those old faces. Every year you'd send hand-drawn or painted birthday cards to people like Mr. Gentry."

She gave a small shrug. "Well, I just—"

"No. Let me finish." He came around to face her fully. "For years, you've worked to keep your relationship with your mom even when she was pulling away. You took Kim out for ice cream when her boyfriend broke up with her. And then you pushed the jerk right into the trash can when you saw him in the school cafeteria." He mildly chuckled at the memory.

"I got detention," she whispered.

"You let Olivia have a shoulder to cry on when her uncle died. And you made me laugh for the first time when my little brother Timothy was sick in the hospital for weeks when I thought I'd never crack a smile again."

Charlotte used her palm to wipe her damp cheek.

"And you didn't do all that because you knew or didn't know who your father was. You did it because you are someone special. Do you know how many phone calls I got from your friends after you got back asking if you were okay? Matt even called."

Her eyes widened.

"He asked if you were okay. And Matt doesn't care about anybody. That's the kind of person you are . . . who's got something special. You have people who care about you."

Charlotte's gaze dropped to the grass, disbelief written across her face.

Jason gently lifted her chin, and she met his gaze. "And so what if you don't know what you want to be yet. That doesn't make you incomplete or worthless. That makes you a teenager."

She bit her lip.

"You've helped a lot of people, but I think it's time you focus on helping yourself. Why don't you focus on enjoying being Charlotte. Because you aren't worthless or not enough. You never have been. I hope you can start seeing it for yourself."

Her voice was barely a whisper. "I want to believe you."

He pulled her into his chest, holding her tight as she softly cried. "Well, I'll just have to keep reminding you." He brushed a hand gently through her hair.

As the sun set, Charlotte sat on her front porch, replaying everything Jason had said. She hugged the chair pillow against her chest while Mr. Culver's blue pickup drove by. Jason's words had struck a nerve. Maybe because they were true, and she didn't want them to be. Squeezing her eyes shut, she shook her head. Was he right? Had this whole time spent searching for her father been a fool's errand? If so, she'd been wrong and that was hard to admit when she already felt lower than a snail dragging itself through the dirt.

Jason said she was already someone special.

Was that true? She didn't feel it.

Jason mentioned that her friends had been calling, asking about her. They cared. Did that mean something? The thought was hard to wrap her head around. Charlotte let out a long sigh and tried to believe what Jason had said. She was *someone.* She mattered to people. The voices of Britney and her posse rose up in protest. So did her grandma's voice, saying she was incomplete.

But now, somehow, Jason's voice rose above them all.

She thought of the time she took Kim for ice cream, how she sat and listened while her friend cried and ranted about the breakup. Dumping Kim's ex in the trash can was an angry impulse, but did sitting and listening count for anything?

She remembered making cookies for Olivia after her uncle died. They cried together, watched their movie, ate too many cookies, and laughed at fond stories of her uncle. He was a cool guy. Did being there like that make her enough?

A smile reached her lips at the memories of the seniors' faces at the nursing home, brightening whenever she brought treats and fudge. Afternoons were spent playing card games and bingo with them. They were lonely, and she wanted to help them feel a little less lonely. That didn't make someone important, did it?

Timothy came to mind and her chest tightened. For weeks, he'd been in the hospital sick with a serious virus. All she could think to do was bake Jason's favorite oatmeal raisin cookies. She hadn't expected him to remember, but he had.

Did these simple acts really matter to anyone?

Her mom's voice drifted back to her—not the distant one she knew so well, but the broken one from the porch. *I missed her so much.* Charlotte swallowed hard. Her mom hadn't pulled away because Charlotte wasn't enough. She'd been afraid, trying to prove something to a town that never stopped judging. And all this time, Charlotte had believed it was her fault.

Aunt Becky's words followed. *Give her the answers she's been looking for.* Maybe the truth wasn't meant to hurt her. Maybe it was something that could heal her and her mom.

Charlotte adjusted herself in the wicker chair as another memory surfaced. The best moments with her mom always happened in the kitchen, baking muffins or eating waffles. Charlotte with her glass of milk, her mom with wine. They'd giggle and talk about movies, boys, and more boys. As she grew older, those moments faded. She wondered if that distance had chipped away her sense of worth.

Jesse Holt's birthday flashed through her mind. He said she had made his day more special. Charlotte shook the thought away before the tears started again. Her eyes hurt.

She squeezed the pillow tighter and rocked gently as her mind spun. She cared for people. She showed it through food and through presence. And somehow, they saw value in her long before she ever had.

Jason said she didn't need to know what she wanted to be yet. Jesse said the same thing. She brushed her cheek against the pillow as tears formed.

She liked food and taking care of people. But that was it. Was that enough for now?

Charlotte grimaced, then nodded gently. Maybe it was all she needed. Maybe it was all right not to have all the answers yet.

A hitch in her throat burned. Tears streamed down her face, but they weren't tears of sadness. They were tears of acceptance. Not having all the answers didn't make her incomplete. It didn't pause her life or diminish her worth.

Charlotte blew out a long, slow breath. After believing the lies for so long, this new truth would take time to accept. She'd have to repeat it until it stuck. Jason could help with that.

Her father was dead. And realizing that didn't change her. It didn't hollow her out or fill her with something new. Jason was right. Putting blame on her uncertainty on not knowing her father had been a convenient shield. His absence didn't define her. His identity didn't have to influence her decisions in life.

Resting her chin in her palm, she shook her head. All this time, she'd missed what was right in front of her. It wasn't her father who shaped her, it was everyone around her.

Her mom's stubbornness lived in her. After all, she'd flown halfway across the country to get answers, for goodness' sake. And her mom flew halfway across the country to find her.

Her grandpa painted at the community fairs, and now the two of them painted and sketched together. Her grandma taught her how to bake when she was two years old, which inspired her to build friendships at the senior center. Jason, goofy and carefree, helped her drop all pretenses.

She hadn't seen it. She'd been whole all along, but each of them shaped how that wholeness took form. Through them, she learned about herself more clearly. They didn't complete her; they gave her weight, direction, and a reason to keep becoming.

She smiled.

Chapter 20

A Family

The sweet fragrance of melted chocolate hung in the air. Charlotte pulled a batch of chocolate chip muffins out of the oven. All those thoughts of food had made her nostalgic—and hungry for the first time since she got back. Pavarotti sang through the stereo. Opera didn't totally suck anymore. At least she had taken a liking to Pavarotti. It was a start. Olivia would be so proud.

Painful as it was to think of him, even Jesse taught her something. Whether intentional or not, he taught her to be more open-minded and think more deeply. Because of it, she'd come around to the idea of maybe trying sushi. But it still sounded gross.

She placed the muffin tin on a hot pad on the kitchen island as the screen door screeched open.

Her mom was home.

Charlotte hissed as melted chocolate got on her thumb, and she stuck her finger in her mouth to soothe it.

"Hey." Her mom entered the kitchen and dropped her purse on the table.

"Hi." Charlotte went to the sink to cool her finger off further.

"Opera, huh?"

"I've grown to like it. A little." She turned off the stereo.

"How are you doing?" Lori leaned on the island.

Charlotte paused before nodding. "Better."

"Well. You're baking. And talking to me. That's a good sign." Hope shone in Lori's eyes as she smiled at her daughter. Removing her hair clip, her mom let her hair tumble past her shoulders and grinned at the baked goodies. "You made chocolate chip muffins. Everything's better with chocolate chips." Mother and daughter each poured their preferred drink and took up seats around the island.

Clinking glasses, they drank, and Charlotte pulled the hot tin closer. "It's gonna take some time, but I'm trying to put things in perspective." She gingerly peeled the hot liner off a muffin and broke off a piece.

Lori did the same. "These are so warm and gooey."

"Tons of sugar and chocolate," Charlotte agreed.

Lori tucked a stray lock behind her daughter's ear, and they shared a reassuring grin, eating in comfortable silence.

"Where's Aunt Becky?"

"She is visiting some old haunts with some old friends."

"I forgot she used to live here. And you didn't go?"

Lori nudged her daughter's shoulder. "I'd rather be here with you."

Charlotte smiled, eating in silence until her last bite. "So do you think now you'll tell me those stories you and Aunt Becky hinted at the other night? After-parties? Hitchhiking? Mom, I'm shocked." With a sparkle in her eyes, she scolded her playfully.

Lori finished her muffin. "Well, I thought we could start with this." She fetched a fat, worn photo album from the table. "Aunt Becky brought me this photo album."

"I saw it."

"This is another one." She flipped through a few of the pages, revealing photos of other band members they'd posed with, images of bands on stage, and pictures of her mom and Becky together on the beaches or driving. Each page documented a passing of time.

"I thought we could go through it, and I could tell you about me and—" She paused on a page with several pictures of a man with long, dark hair.

Charlotte leaned closer to a photo, studying the face that mirrored her own. The man's features were smooth and round with a thick mustache. His smile outshone anyone else in the picture. His nose wrinkled just like hers. Were his eyes brown or hazel?

In most of the pictures, he wore beaded jackets and flared pants, tinted circular glasses perched on his nose, and often held a cigarette in his left hand.

"And I could tell you about your father."

There were pages of them together, standing beside a minivan, laughing with friends in a field at an outdoor concert. One image stood out—her mother leaning into her father, laughing straight into the camera. Her father, arms wrapped tightly around her, wasn't looking at the lens, but at her mom, smiling with complete adoration.

Charlotte looked up at her mom. "I'd like that a lot."

Toward the end of the week, Charlotte planned to host a dinner and spent all day cooking and baking. When the doorbell announced her guests' arrival, she swung open the door with a gasp of delight.

The Hunter family stood on the porch with bright and cheery greetings. But one thing was different. Jason. His shaggy hair was all gone, cut short and spiked. He looked like a new person.

He'd always been handsome, but this version was something else entirely. Charlotte swallowed, and her pulse quickened.

"Your hair! It's all gone," Charlotte exclaimed.

Mrs. Hunter chuckled. "He got it done yesterday. It makes him look all grown-up."

"I think it makes him look stupid," Timothy muttered and received a whack on the head from his brother.

"Hello, hello." Aunt Becky glided into the front room and ushered them inside, while Lori led them into the dining room. Thank goodness, the Hunters' presence would make conversation much easier. Her grandparents had arrived earlier and, given their opinion of Aunt Becky, the atmosphere in the house had been interesting to say the least, polite yet chilly. Charlotte had a sneaking suspicion that if she hadn't been there, their conversations would've turned into arguing.

After high-fiving Mr. Hunter, Charlotte attempted to poke Timothy in the side as he walked past, but he dodged it, retaliating with a playful shove.

"I got my eye on you," she said.

Timothy cackled, trailing after his parents into the room with the food.

Idle chatter drifted in from the dining room, while Charlotte and Jason lingered behind. An awkward moment stretched between them until he finally said, "So what do you think?" He gestured to his head.

"It's different. I like it. A lot." A faint blush rose to her cheeks, while Jason grinned and looked at the floor.

Silence again.

She had a lot she wanted to say. There was a lot she wanted to apologize for and a lot she wanted to thank him for. However, despite how much she'd practiced, the words didn't form. Charlotte glanced at the coffee table and went over to the plate of cookies sitting there. She held up a cookie. "I made your favorite. Kind of a peace offering."

"Thanks."

"Jason, I'm so sorry—" but she was cut off by his lips pressing on hers. Confident but gentle.

He pulled back with his signature grin, grabbed the cookie from her hand, and took a bite. "I've been wanting to do that for a while."

Charlotte stood still.

Stunned.

What just happened?

But what was even more shocking was that all she could think about was how soft his lips were, how right it felt to be kissed by him. Her cheeks grew warm. Why did they do that? She touched her cheek and cleared her throat.

"Thank you." Instantly, she frowned. Those weren't the right words to say.

He laughed. "You're welcome."

His smile. A month ago, that smile would have struck her as goofy.

Now it didn't. Aside from the afternoon at the park, it had been over a month since they had seen each other. How could he have changed so much? With his short hair, he seemed to have shed his boyish look and changed into something new. And it was very attractive.

She didn't quite know what to do, so she shoved his arm. "I heard your mom and my mom discuss your involvement in all this. How much trouble did I get you in?"

"Yard work and no skateboarding for the next two weeks."

Charlotte hissed, "Yikes. Sorry."

"I've had worse. You?"

She scrunched her nose. "Volunteer at the next lady's luncheon. I have to serve everyone, including Britney and her squad."

"You have it worse." Jason took her hand and laced his fingers through hers as they walked toward the kitchen.

"Jase? Thanks. Thanks for always seeing me for who I am."

"Anytime." He smiled, and her cheeks grew warm.

What the heck was happening?

There was no weirdness or tension as they held hands. The familiar, comfortable connection they always shared flowed between them. They didn't have to say anything. At least, not right now. Holding her best friend's hand was more than all right. It was right.

Lori instructed everyone on the buffet displayed on the counters, and Charlotte hung back to let the guests dish up. Her grandad talked with Mr. Hunter about the latest news, and the women discussed the upcoming potluck before the school season and the dishes they planned on bringing. Jason smacked Timothy in the back of the head, and Timothy retaliated with a jab to his brother's side.

Their antics made Charlotte giggle. The Hunters had been there her whole life, through thick and thin. All the scraped knees, the Christmases, the tough decisions, the tears, and the laughter. And they happily accepted this dinner invitation. They weren't like family—they were family.

Charlotte smiled at the realization. A family had been right here all along. Gratitude washed over her.

" . . . Charlotte did most of the cooking all day today. She's always been so good at putting together flavors and menus," Lori said.

"Oh, wow. Charlotte, I'm impressed," Mrs. Hunter commented as they settled around the table.

Just as Charlotte sat down with her family, the doorbell rang. "Who could that be?"

Lori and Becky exchanged looks before her mom shrugged, hiding a smile. "Why don't you go find out?"

Charlotte eyed her suspiciously before going to the door. Opening it, she froze. Jesse Holt was standing on her front porch.

"Hi." He smiled.

"Hi." Her voice cracked, and she cleared her throat. "You're here." A wave of embarrassment swept through her, and she kicked the threshold nervously.

He nodded. "Yes, I am."

"In South Carolina."

"Yes."

"Why?"

"You. All summer I got to know this pretty amazing girl. We shared pie, played guitars, and then suddenly she disappeared."

"I'm sorry I put you through everything I did."

He took a step closer. "I'm not. I'm glad I met you. The problem is I can't seem to get you out of my head." He grinned, then grew serious. "I'm sorry I'm not your father. I would've been over the moon to have a daughter like you."

Lori joined them at the front door, and Jesse greeted her warmly.

He turned back to Charlotte. "The band, we've decided to cool it for a while. The Bowl was our last engagement. After that, no new album. I'm not going on tour anytime soon."

Charlotte's expression widened. "You gave it up?"

"Let's say we've put things on pause. At least for now."

"But you love playing for the crowds."

"It hasn't been fun for a while."

"Then what are you going to do?"

Jesse smiled at Lori before looking back at Charlotte. "I was thinking of an extended vacation. Here in South Carolina. I've heard it's a nice town."

Charlotte flung her arms around his neck. He stumbled back a little, laughing as he hugged her tight.

"Besides, Greenville isn't too far from here, and I've been told it's a great place to experience vibrant new music."

Lori spoke up, "We'd love it if you'd join us for dinner. We have plenty of room."

"Oh, yes. Please. Please, yes." Charlotte took his arm.

"I'd have to be crazy to turn down a home-cooked, Southern meal. I'd love to." Jesse grinned sheepishly and was welcomed inside.

When Lori went to shut the door, he attempted to help. Their hands both touched the doorknob, then recoiled. "Sorry," she said awkwardly and went into the dining room.

Charlotte started to follow, still holding his arm, but he hung back.

"There is one thing."

Charlotte frowned. "What's up?"

He crimped his lips, and his tone grew serious. "The band. They're a bit upset with you."

Charlotte's heart fluttered. "Oh, no. Why? What'd I do?"

He stifled a grin. "You owe them an article."

All fears quickly washed away, and Charlotte playfully socked him in the arm. "Don't do that. You had me genuinely worried. But a promise is a promise. I will write one up for you all. Maybe I can get extra credit from Ms. Talbot, my actual teacher."

"J. J. might know a few editorials he could send it to. You could get published."

"Whoa. That'd be so cool."

"Now, the band wants it honest but favorable. And Danny and Scott need a lot of flowery words to describe them. Their egos are fragile."

Charlotte poked Jesse in the rib.

"Ah! Okay, okay. Roy says hi and don't be a stranger." He slung an arm around her shoulders and gave a tight squeeze.

"Hi there, handsome. Thought for sure you'd bring a certain lead singer with you." Aunt Becky flashed a dazzling grin at the musician.

Charlotte's grandparents rolled their eyes.

"Nice to see you again, Becky." He shook hands as he was introduced around the room.

"And this is Jason." Charlotte put a hand on her best friend's shoulder.

"*The* Jason? Nice to meet you, man."

Jason was a little flustered at meeting the celebrity but firmly shook his hand. "Thanks for the signed album."

Lori dished him a plate, and they all sat down to dinner. Conversation and laughter filled the evening. This was her family, and being among them made her so happy that she felt like she might burst.

Late one summer night, in the quiet house, a deep sense of contentment filled Charlotte's heart and she reached for a pen and paper.

Ms. Talbot,

You asked me what I wanted to be when I graduated. What can be a seemingly simple question to one can terrify another. I, unfortunately, was the latter. At the beginning of the summer of 1994, I was terrified of this question because of the other questions it brought to the surface. These uncertainties and unknowns led me on a search for the truth about family, facing my fears, and finding my self-worth.

What do I want to be when I graduate? At the beginning of the summer, I was terrified to answer this question. Now with summer coming to a close, I'm beginning to understand how to respond.

What to "be" and "do" for the future, asked from a purely career standpoint, is still up for debate. However, daydreaming and the discovering process of exploring different career paths has been highly enjoyable. Imagining is a true first for me. From baking, learning to play the guitar, and understanding the ins and outs of classic sports cars, it has been a wild experience.

While this was truly one of the hardest summers I've ever faced, it was also one of the best. The search for who I want to be led me to start with answering the question of who I am. I've learned a few new truths.

Even though my biological father wasn't in my life, this summer I met someone who began to fill that role. He hasn't been here long, but in that short time, he's supported me and taught me things I never thought I'd learn. From baking together and sitting on the porch talking to taking long walks around our little town, he's helped me feel less alone. Because of him, I can proudly say I know how to change the oil in a car, change a tire, and am still working on replacing brake pads.

I'm focusing on "being" me, Charlotte Reynolds. Who she is fully has yet to be determined, but I'm learning to enjoy the unknown. I'm learning to accept it's all right not to know all the answers.

In closing, on my way to answer your question, I found a family. I faced my fears and found out I'm a pretty cool person, and I'm excited to see what the next summer holds for me. For now, what I want to be isn't nearly as important as who I am.

Epilogue

The Rest of the Summer

In the final weeks of summer vacation, writing the band's editorial article took longer than expected. Jason and Charlotte spent more time giggling over nothing and holding hands rather than pencils. And she discovered the beautiful sparkle in Jason's eyes.

When they did look through her travel notes, they relived the experiences, and she relayed memories to Jason. One day, they'd go to California together, and she'd show him everything.

Once the article was completed, they walked hand in hand to the post office to send it to the band's manager.

Oak Falls' town potluck was the first time she introduced Jesse to the community. Preparing for it was a series of comedic events as Jesse turned everything from measuring out the flour to attempting to crack an egg into a goofy performance.

It might have been a teensy bit selfish on Charlotte's part, but she loved every minute of driving up to the potluck in a red 1970 Ford Mustang with her mom, Aunt Becky, and Jesse. Her aunt planned to stay for the rest of the summer, not wanting to miss hanging with Jesse Holt.

Their arrival didn't go unnoticed. Britney and her friends watched as Jesse helped Charlotte and the women out of the car. The look on Britney's face was the cherry on top.

It felt so wrong, yet so good, to see her nemesis brought down a peg or two. To make it even better, Britney's mom, Mrs. Abernathy, surprised everyone by fawning over Jesse and gushing about being a fan of the band back in the day. Britney practically crumbled with embarrassment.

The evening had one more surprise when Matt Kendrick stepped out of his family's car. Charlotte threw her arms around his neck. "What are you doing here?"

He grimaced as he stepped back. "I have family here, remember? I can come visit whenever I want."

A huge smile wrinkled her nose. "You wanted to check up on me. You flew across the country to see if I was all right."

"Don't think so highly of yourself."

"Because we're friends. Admit it."

He answered with a shy smile and a shake of the head before walking away to catch up with old friends.

No icy rejection. A genuine smile. Mission complete, and it felt so good.

Aunt Becky headed back home to LA. It was hard to say goodbye, but they promised to keep in touch more.

In the living room, Charlotte and Jesse sat on the floor around the coffee table with a half-eaten pizza and the sprawled-out photo albums. Lori sat on the couch behind them as they reminisced of the days gone by. It had not gone unnoticed to Charlotte the subtle touches or lingering glances her mother and Jesse had developed. She never brought attention to it, but her insides were doing handsprings.

When they got to the pictures of Lori and Jesse, he stopped.

"Wait a minute, that is you? You're *that* Lori?"

"What other Lori would I be?"

"I *remember* you."

Charlotte smacked her mom's leg. "He remembers you! Wait, he *remembers* you. Why did he say it like that? Why did you say it like that? Mom, what did you do?"

"Nothing. It's time for bed." Lori tried to snatch the photograph from his hand. He skillfully evaded her desperate grasps.

"It's only eight-thirty on a Saturday. Jesse, tell me. What did she do?"

She turned to her mom. "And don't think for one minute that I won't hold it over your head till the end of time."

He grinned. "I remember thinking she was hot."

Charlotte laughed, and Lori blushed. "I know my mom thought the same thing about you."

"Okay, that's enough."

"Do you want to hear about what happened in San Diego or the first time I met your mom?"

Charlotte gasped as her eyes danced. "Um . . . the first time you met, of course."

"Oh, no." Lori buried her head.

"Oh, yes."

"Do tell." Charlotte leaned in.

"Don't say it," Lori pleaded.

"It was an after-party in San Francisco. There were scores of chicks trying to get at us. Your mom, I don't know how she did it, but she blew past all of them and our security in her patchwork halter top and tight denim jeans that flared at the bottom. Before I knew what was happening, she pinned me against the wall and attacked me."

"No way!"

"That's not what happened," Lori cried out. "I didn't attack you."

"You had your leg wrapped around mine," he teased. "Her hands were all over me. I had to pry her lips off my own."

"Mommmm," Charlotte scolded.

Lori spoke from behind her hands, "This is so embarrassing."

"Now, I gotta know about San Diego."

"No!" Lori put her hand over Jesse's mouth just as he was about to speak.

The Fall

The news of Jason and her updating their status to officially boyfriend and girlfriend swept through the whole school. And as the months went by, it was heartwarming to come home from school to find Jesse and her mom giggling over wine like a couple of lovestruck high schoolers, much like her and Jason.

"Mom, are you playing hooky? Skipping on work?"

Lori straightened. "Not completely. I did just sell Jesse a house."

Charlotte gasped. "Really? You're gonna move out here?"

"I'll still have my home on the Coast. I think I'll bounce back and forth. You both are more than welcome to come with me."

Charlotte's eyes sparkled at the prospect. "Inviting us out to your California place? Sounds like you two are getting close," she teased.

Jesse volleyed it right back. "I could say the same about you and Jason. I've seen the way you two look at each other."

"Are you two official yet?"

"Yep, we've upgraded to boyfriend and girlfriend."

"Congratulations," Jesse said.

"That's great, honey." Lori's smile faded, and she leaned forward in earnest. "Just how serious is it between you two?"

"I haven't attacked him or anything."

Jesse snorted and received a glare from Lori.

"Mom, don't worry, we're taking it slow."

Lori sighed dramatically. "Oh, thank the Lord. You take it as slow as possible."

Thanksgiving was spent with Jesse's family in California. Charlotte and Jason had a long and dramatic goodbye at the airport, so much so that her mom had to drag her away. She knew it seemed ridiculous since they were apart for so long over the summer, but things were different now. She would miss Jason terribly.

They stayed at Jesse's gorgeous hilltop home, a modern six-bedroom with a sweeping view, a barely used kitchen, and a huge garage full of cars. Lori practically slobbered at the real estate, and Charlotte admired his massive guitar collection. To her complete shock, he confessed to owning at least two hundred guitars.

This holiday was going to be eye-opening. It was the first time they'd be meeting Jesse's large family. It was exciting to get to know more about Jesse the brother and uncle, rather than Jesse the rock star.

As excited as Charlotte was to meet the family, her mom was just as nervous. A few hours before they were to drive over to the Holts' house, Charlotte found her mom in a bathroom draped over the toilet. "You all right?"

"No," her mom moaned.

"You're not pregnant, are you?"

"Absolutely not."

"Oh, good." Charlotte breathed a dramatic sigh of relief. "Are you sick?"

"No, Charlotte. I'm about to meet the Holts."

"And it has you puking into the toilet?"

"I'm the groupie who was infatuated with their son."

Charlotte pursed her lips. "Yeah, you kind of were."

Lori groaned.

Charlotte hoisted her mom to her feet. "But now you are a successful real estate agent who's lived a nice, stable, boring life."

Lori winced at her reflection in the mirror.

"Now, wash your face, brush your teeth, and pull yourself together. It'll be great."

Despite Lori's nerves, the holiday was lovely with the whole family together. Charlotte took pity on her mom and stuck close to her all evening, never letting Jesse's mother get her alone. Charlotte especially loved his family and gathered stories from his brothers that she could use for blackmail later.

The New Year

Christmas was spent together in their whimsical fairy-tale hometown, and Charlotte loved showing it off to Jesse. Waking up on Christmas morning sharing it with him and her mom was a dream come true.

The following year became a whirlwind, beginning with a phone call. When Charlotte answered, a big grin appeared on her face. "Roy! It's nice to hear your voice."

After a quick catch-up and Roy announcing his engagement, she passed the phone to Jesse. From what Charlotte could tell, the entire band was on the other end. They talked for a while, and when Jesse hung up, he informed them of news that the band was getting back together.

Saying goodbye was hard, even harder for Lori, but they promised it wouldn't be long. Soon couldn't come fast enough. Over spring break, Charlotte checked one item off Jason's wish list when Jesse flew them out to California to sit in on their recording sessions. Jason was over the moon meeting the band, especially Roy, who teased Jason mercilessly.

They returned in the summer. Charlotte showed Jason everything, and experiencing it all through him made it feel brand new. They spent time with Aunt Becky, ate burgers with Matt, Charlotte paid, and they swapped stories.

And when Caravan launched their new album, they were seated in the front row on opening night of their tour.

Graduation Day

But the best day of her life was one evening when she walked into the kitchen to find balloons, flowers, a present, cards, and muffins on the counter. Jesse and her mom shouted, "Happy graduation!"

"Thanks." She smelled the fragrant roses and opened several of the cards from the band members offering congratulations. The one from Roy was so hilarious that she laughed out loud.

"What's going on?" she asked with a mouthful of muffin. "You two are smiling like Cheshire cats."

Her mom kept wiping tears from her eyes, even though she was grinning from ear to ear.

The two exchanged looks before Lori held out her hand to show a glittering diamond ring. Charlotte covered her mouth. "No way!" She screamed and hugged her mom, jumping up and down. "I'm so happy for you both. I want details." Happy tears fell down her cheeks. "This is the best present."

"That was surprise number one." Jesse gestured to the present on the counter.

Charlotte raised her brow and unwrapped the box. Opening the lid, she stared at the contents inside. A stack of papers she didn't fully understand.

Then she saw it.

She gasped.

Tears gushed.

"Charlotte Reynolds," Jesse said as he came around the island. "Would you do me the greatest honor of allowing me to adopt you officially as my daughter?"

Charlotte hugged him tight. "Yes!"

The End

About the Author

Cherie Wolfe has been writing stories ever since she saw the first *Pirates of the Caribbean* movie in theaters. Upon coming home from the theater, she recited the whole movie to her father and, of course, she holed herself away in her bedroom to write her own pirate adventure. This one epic movie sparked a lifelong passion and dream.

Since then, she has spent countless hours crafting worlds and creating meaningful and heartfelt characters. She developed a love for the art and science behind storytelling. In addition to writing novels, she also writes short skits and plays performed by children in drama classes she teaches on the side. When not writing, she loves cooking and baking, laughing with her husband, and spoiling her godsons.

www.ingramcontent.com/pod-product-compliance
Lightning Source LLC
LaVergne TN
LVHW012048160826
845678LV00014B/2742

* 9 7 8 1 9 6 0 8 1 4 2 4 1 *